LLC

What You Need to Know About Starting a Limited Liability Company along with Tips for Dealing with Bookkeeping, Accounting, and Taxes as a Small Business

Contents

Introduction

If you are one of the many highly motivated individuals who are looking to achieve the American dream by owning a business, forming a Limited Liability Company can be a great way to organize your company. This form of business structure has become one of the most popular in the U.S. because of its many advantages.

An LLC requires fewer formalities to start, protects you and your personal assets, and above all, offers tax flexibility. But don't take my word for it just yet. I will begin this book with an overview of the various business structures available to you and go over the main reasons an LLC is perhaps the best option. Whether you are just starting out as an entrepreneur or you have your own company established already, this book will help you understand why an LLC business may be the best option for you.

This book is divided into three sections for easy understanding and clarity. Part one contains in-depth information about the essentials of what a Limited Liability Company is and the various forms of LLC business structures available.

In part two, we zoom in on the process of forming a Limited Liability Company. If you are won over already on the idea of establishing your business as an LLC, this chapter contains a handy guide that takes you through the process. It will highlight the process of starting an LLC from scratch or converting an already-existing business to a Limited Liability Company. Part two also contains information about basic LLC formation processes, such as choosing the right name for your business, creating the articles of organization, and the LLC operating agreement, which is a vital document that establishes your business as an LLC.

This book is an A to Z guide on forming and running your own Limited Liability Company. Part three covers in detail the various processes involved in the day to day running of a Limited Liability Company. You will find information about how to do accounting for your LLC, preparing financial statements, and doing taxes for an LLC.

All the information contained in this book is designed to help you to build a Limited Liability Company that thrives and complies with all the regulations and standards. So whether your mind is already made up to start a Limited Liability Company or you still need some convincing, follow along as I show you, step-by-step, how easy creating your own Limited Liability Company can be.

PART ONE: LLC Business Essentials

Chapter One: What is an LLC?

For anyone planning to start a business, one of the major decisions they face is deciding on its organizational structure. This decision is important because the business structure will determine the income, liability implications, tax accounting, and other important details pertaining to the business.

Types of Business Structures

In the United States, there are four major business structures. They are sole proprietorship, partnership, corporation, and limited liability. We start by explaining each of these business structures as a simple guide to prospective business owners.

Sole Proprietorship

Most businesses that have just one owner typically start as a sole proprietorship. Many become nothing else. But many sole proprietorships grow and eventually become organized into other forms of business structures. Starting a business as a sole proprietor is a relatively simple process. You need not have any official government paper or have your company registered with the IRS. This is because a sole proprietorship isn't a taxable business entity. People who own a sole proprietorship simply need to add a profit and loss from business form (Schedule C form) to their personal tax returns, and they have things covered.

A sole proprietorship has the simplest business organization structure possible. This business structure gives total control of the company operations to the owner. Usually, they are home-based companies, small shops, one-person consulting firms, or simple retail businesses. A sole proprietor is responsible for the day to day running of the business. He or she handles activities like record-keeping, doing taxes (self-employment taxes), and decision making. This form of business structure provides no protection for the business owner. He or she is held liable for the company's financial obligations and debt.

Partnership

Any business started and ran by one or more persons is considered a partnership by the IRS. With a partnership, each person (partner) is considered equally liable. For businesses with more than one owner, a partnership is the most flexible structure you can go for.

Like sole proprietorships, partnerships are not taxable entities. Rather, each partner has to file his or her own income on their personal tax return and pay self-employment tax to the IRS. The partners also share joint liability. This means they are responsible for debts, financial obligations, and even for the actions of their partners in terms of the business. Partnerships can be formed simply through oral agreement and handshakes. However, a written legal agreement is the best option, as this will be helpful with lawsuits and disputes between partners.

Partnerships can be structured in two ways, either as a general partnership or limited partnership. In general partnerships, all partners pool their resources together to form the business, and they all participate in running the business. With limited partnerships, not all the partners participate in running the business. One partner actively takes control of business activities while the other(s) is or are only partners because of their financial contribution to the company.

Corporations

Corporations are businesses that operate as separate legal entities from their owners. Hence, the owners are protected from claims filed against the activities of the company or debts. However, the obligations of incorporating a company are enormous and significant resources will be required to pay for legal and accounting activities.

A corporation is the most complex form of organizational structure for any business. Typically, corporations are regulated by the laws of the state where they are set up. Unlike partnerships and a sole proprietorship, they are taxed as separate entities from the owner(s) by the IRS.

Corporations can be structured in two ways, either as S-corporations or C-corporations. This categorization is based on the way the corporations are organized in terms of taxation.

• **S Corporation:** Subchapter S corporations have less than 100 shareholders. They function more like partnerships because the income and loss of the company may be passed on to the shareholders to avoid paying federal taxes. However, the owners of the business have legal protection and are immune from corporate liabilities.

• **Subchapter C Corporation:** Ordinary corporations are regarded as subchapter C corporations. They are considered separate legal entities, and the tax returns are filed separately from shareholders. Because a C-corporation is a legal entity, in court it is treated more or less like a person.

Limited Liability Company (LLC)

A Limited Liability Company is a relatively new form of business structure. It falls somewhere in-between all the other business structures. It is organized in the form of a sole proprietorship or partnership but offers a level of legal protection similar to that of a corporation.

In most states, owners (members) of an LLC get legal protection from liability or lawsuits. They are not required to pay corporate taxes (unless they elect to do so) or go through every registration requirement of a corporation. They are essentially treated as sole proprietorship or partnership business unless they specifically request to be taxed as a corporation.

What is a Limited Liability Company?

Although it is the newest form of business structure, limited liability companies have become one of the most popular in the world. This is a sort of hybrid company. It combines the liability protection of an incorporated company with the tax advantages of a sole proprietorship or partnership business.

A Limited Liability Company is relatively easier to form compared to a corporation. The tax obligations flow down to the owners of the business (referred to as members in this case) who pay the taxes as personal taxes instead of corporate taxes.

The term "limited liability (LLC)" is used to refer to the specific form of private limited company practiced in the United States.

What is a limited company? In a limited company, the members bear a liability limited to their individual investment in the company. Limited companies are typically of two forms. They can be limited by guarantee or by shares. Limited companies limited by shares can be private or public companies. There are laws and rules in every country and state that govern who may become a member of a private limited company. But anyone can become a member of a public limited company by simply buying shares in the company. Although limited companies exist in different countries, each country has its own rules governing operation and organization.

Now that you are familiar with what a limited company is let's go back to our definition of a Limited Liability Company.

A Limited Liability Company combines the pass-through taxation structure of a sole proprietorship or partnership with the limited liability of a corporation. Under state laws, it is considered a corporation because the members are covered by limited liability. This business structure is well known for the flexibility it offers business owners to choose the tax rules under which the company will operate. An LLC may choose to operate under corporate tax rules where tax is charged in the form of corporate tax. They may also choose to be treated as partnerships with the tax charged as income tax for the members. In some cases, LLCs may even be organized as NPOs (Non-Profit Organizations.)

Although a common business structure, the limited liability structure is not open for all businesses. Companies that offer professional services that require state licenses may not be allowed to operate as LLCs. This includes companies offering legal or medical services. Such companies are only allowed to form a Professional Limited Liability Company, which is still similar to an LLC.

A Limited Liability Company is an unincorporated business. Hence, it is distinct from a corporation. Still, it shares a primary characteristic of a corporation in terms of limited liability. At the same time, it has the pass-through income taxation characteristics of a sole proprietorship (if it is owned by just one person) or that of a partnership (if it is owned by more than one person). Generally, operating an LLC is a more flexible form of business organization than a corporation. It is a business structure that is better suited to companies with one owner.

Besides the different tax laws governing both entities, LLCs and corporations are also described by different distinct terms. For instance, we don't say an LLC is "Incorporated" when it is formed. Rather, the term "organized" is used. Similarly, while the founding documents of a corporation are referred to as "Articles of Incorporation," those of an LLC are called "Articles of Organization."

Limited liability companies don't have "by-laws." Instead, the internal operations of the company are governed by an "operating agreement." The owners of the company are not called shareholders. They are members with membership interest or LLC interests measured in units or percentages (instead of shares). The legal document that represents the ownership right of members of a Limited Liability Company is known as a "membership".

Types of LLCs

The Limited Liability Company structure is one of the commonest business forms in the United States. LLCs can be structured in various ways, depending on various factors. Some of the most popular forms of organizing an LLC include:

1. Single-Member LLC/Multiple-Member LLC: As the name implies, a single-member Limited Liability Company is a type of LLC that is owned by an individual. Similarly, a multiple-member LLC is a type of LLC that is owned by more than one person. However, it is important to note that forming a single-member or multiple-member Limited Liability Company isn't only a function of the number of owners involved. A business owner will weigh the merits of each system to determine whether to form a single or multi-member LLC.

2. Member-Managed LLC/Manager-Managed LLC: A member-managed Limited Liability Company is run directly by the owner(s) of the business. In the manager-managed LLC structure, a separate manager will be appointed to manage the day-to-day operations of the business.

3. Domestic LLC/ Foreign LLC: Domestic Limited Liability Company refers to an LLC that operates within the state where it is registered. For instance, a company that is registered in Washington and does business in Washington is an example of a domestic LLC. Conversely, a foreign LLC is one that operates in a state outside of where it is registered. "Operating in" a state in this sense means:

● Having a bank account in a bank within the State

● Selling products in the State either directly or through parties directly tied to the company

● Owning property in the state (real estate, a fleet of trucks, etc.

● Having office facilities or holding meetings regularly in the state

4. Restricted LLCs: A restricted liability company is a type of LLC that has some restrictions within the Articles of Organization. Most notably, the members have to wait for ten years before they can receive their distributions from the business.

5. Anonymous LLC: As the name implies, an anonymous Limited Liability Company is an LLC where the details of the owners are kept private from the public. This is a very rare form of LLC.

LLCs may also be categorized based on how they elect to be taxed. An LLC may be taxed as a corporation or like a sole proprietorship. These and the other forms of limited liability companies will be covered in greater detail in chapter three, which will also cover some tips to help you choose the right business structure and options that suit your needs.

Chapter Two: Is an LLC Right for Me?

As a prospective business owner, before deciding to form a Limited Liability Company you need to be familiar with the various options available to you. You should also find out the advantages and disadvantages of a Limited Liability Company. This way, you can compare it with other forms of business structure and make a more informed decision. In this chapter, we will make a brief comparison of limited liability companies with other business entities, considering the specific advantages and disadvantages of each.

Limited liability Companies Compared to Corporations

The main similarity between limited liability companies and corporations is that both business types provide protection for their owners. Hence, this mode of business allows anyone to start a business without having to worry about liability. However, apart from these similarities, creating a Limited Liability Company also comes with some unique advantages over corporations. There are fewer corporate formalities involved in forming and running a Limited

Liability Company. An LLC also offers greater tax flexibility compared to corporations. It has some limitations, as well. Let's examine some of the advantages and limitations of LLCs compared to corporations.

Advantages of an LLC Over Corporations

1. Fewer Formalities: The process of creating a corporation is a very elaborate one; there are a lot of corporate formalities involved. Corporations are obligated to hold regular meetings among shareholders and directors. In these meetings, written records of discussions must be kept and submitted to the State as part of the annual reports. Without this documentation, or if they are not done properly, the "corporate veil" that protects shareholders may become invalidated in case of litigation.

This is not the case with LLCs. The members are not obligated to hold meetings. If they do hold meetings, they do so to keep the business running and not as a matter of obligation. This also means less paperwork is required.

2. Tax Flexibility: A Limited Liability Company is a pass-through tax entity by default. This means the default system of taxation is similar to that of a sole proprietorship or partnership, which helps to avoid double taxation. Only the owners of the company will be required to pay income tax while the company itself is free from any corporate tax liabilities. However, an LLC may choose to pay tax like a corporation.

3. Property Contributions: No matter how much interest an individual has in an LLC, the property contributed by him or her to form an LLC is not taxable. This is not the case with corporations. The IRS frees tax only on property contributors that have higher interest and control of the company, but the contribution of owners with minority interests are taxed.

4. There is No Restriction on Ownership: The membership of a Limited Liability Company can be made up of any number of individuals. But that of a Schedule S corporation is restricted to just a hundred. There is also no limit to the type of individuals the LLC can be made up of.

5. It Allows the Use of the Cash Accounting Method: Unlike C corporations that are only allowed to use the accrual method of accounting, LLCs are allowed to use the cash method of accounting if they choose to. What this means is that the company does not report income until payment has been received in cash, and tax is only paid on cash recorded.

6. Losses Can be Deducted: Managers of a Limited Liability Company can deduct the operating losses of the business from the regular income of the members to a certain legal extent. This may also be possible for some types of corporations, but it does not apply to all types. Shareholders in an S corporation can also deduct the operating losses of the business. However, in the case of a C corporation, this is not possible.

7. Membership Interests Can be Placed in a Living Trust: It is legally permitted for members of an LLC company to put their interests from the business into a living trust. This is not possible with an S corporation. Putting shares in a living trust, in this case, can jeopardize the status of the corporation.

Disadvantages of a Limited Liability Company Compared to a Corporation

1. Medicare and Social Security Taxes are Deducted from the Profits: For a Limited Liability Company that elects to be taxed as a pass-through tax entity, all the earned income of members will be subject to self-employment tax. This means deductions like Medicare taxes and social security taxes will be made from the earnings of the members. This might not be a problem for a big LLC where the members take out large salaries and profit. For instance, for owners with salaries and profits of around $120,000, social security taxation will not apply. However, in the case of a much smaller company, where the owner takes out about $30,000 as salary, and realizes profits of $20,000, up to $3000 will be charged as taxes.

In the case of a corporation, money can be taken either in the form of salary or as dividends, which will be tax-free. To avoid this, an LLC can choose to be taxed as a corporate entity instead.

2. Members of LLCs Must be Able to Recognize Profits Immediately: Again, this applies to LLCs that choose to pay tax like a pass-through entity. Since the profits are distributed automatically as part of the member's income, members will be taxed on the corporation's profits. This is not the case with corporations since the profits are not distributed to shareholders immediately.

3. Members Bear Personal Liability for their Payroll Taxes: If an LLC is taxed like a sole proprietorship or partnership, members of the company can be held liable if the company fails to pay payroll taxes. In the case of a corporate entity, the shareholders are not liable for failure to pay payroll taxes. Only officers and directors in the company will be held liable.

4. Unfavorable Tax Fees and Rules in Some U.S. States: Some states are notorious as regards tax rules for LLCs. They may require limited liability companies to pay more taxes on revenues than corporations are required to pay.

These are some of the advantages and limitations of LLCs compared to corporations. You must consider these merits and detriments when choosing between forming a Limited Liability Company or incorporating.

Next, we compare limited liability companies with sole proprietorship and general partnerships.

LLCs Compared to Sole Proprietorship

Limited liability companies offer even more advantages over partnerships and sole proprietorship. There is little wonder that most partnerships or one-man businesses switch to LLCs. But does that mean an LLC is always a better option? Well, there are instances where choosing to stay as a sole proprietorship business or partnership still makes more business sense. Let's consider the advantages and potential limitations of an LLC.

Advantages of an LLC over Sole Proprietorship

1. Limited Liability: This is, of course, the main advantage of a limited liability business over a one-man company or partnership. In the latter, the owner(s) of the business bear complete liability for the business. In cases of litigation, creditors are legally empowered to go after their assets and confiscate them. An LLC offers greater protection for members from such liabilities. Creditors cannot hold the bank accounts, real estate, or any other property of members of an LLC to pay for debts owed by the company. The only risk is with the initial investment contributed by the members into the business. The personal assets of the owners are not in any way affected in case of bankruptcy.

It is important to note that a Limited Liability Company cannot protect members who accrue debts through negligence or by standing as a guarantor for the company. Also, only LLCs formed and operated through the proper legal formalities such as filing of annual reports, keeping separate bank records, and so on will be protected under the law.

2. Continuous Existence: An LLC has a longer lifespan compared to a sole proprietorship or partnership. We could say that a Limited Liability Company has a perpetual lifespan. A sole-proprietorship's lifespan is virtually the same as that of its founder or partners. If they die, and the assets of the business are transferred to their heirs, that may very well be the end of the business, unless the heirs opt to continue it.

Even if the new owners decide to continue the business in their own names, it will be considered an entirely new business entity under the law even if they are making use of assets from the former business.

This is because the new owners will have to get new licenses, register under a new name, and get new tax numbers, among other things. This is virtually the same as starting a new business from scratch. With an LLC, the business can still continue to operate with the former licenses even after the demise of a member.

3. **LLCs are Easily Transferable:** It is quite easy to transfer a Limited Liability Company, including all its assets and accounts to a new owner. This is done by simply assigning a stake in the company to the new owner. With a sole proprietorship or partnership, the process is much more elaborate. Assets, accounts, permits, and licenses must be transferred individually to the new owner.

For instance, if John decided to sell his Limited Liability Company to Jack, Jack does not have to apply for a new business license or change the titles on the real estate and other assets of the business. All of these are already in the company name and will remain the same, even if ownership of the business changes.

4. **Profits Can be Shared Without Losing Ownership:** For a sole proprietorship, sharing profits requires the owner to give up some control of the business. With an LLC, profit and ownership are separated. It is possible to set up a share of profit independent of the share of ownership on the business. For example, John, who is a member of an LLC, may assign a portion of his or her profit to his children. These children can be made members of the company, giving them a share of the company without actually allowing them control over the company.

5. **Capital Can be Raised Easily:** Another benefit of a Limited Liability Company over a single-owner business is the fact that capital can be raised easily through loans or by admitting new members into the company. In many cases, an LLC will not have to pay tax on money raised by selling part of the company's share. This, along with the fact that shares can be easily sold while the owners retain control of the business, makes it easy to raise money from willing investors. However, the process of selling interests in an LLC is a thoroughly guarded one, with strict rules and serious punishments for violators.

6. Separate Record-Keeping: For a Limited Liability Company, the company's financial record and bank account are kept separate from those of the owner. This reduces the stress in differentiating between the expenses and other financial details of the business and those of the owner in a sole proprietorship.

7. Ease of Estate Planning: Given its similarities to a corporation, a Limited Liability Company is a more organized business entity. Hence ownership and management are better arranged compared to how it operates in partnerships or sole proprietorship. In the case of an LLC, members can be assigned percentages and given control individually. Members who are incapable or simply not interested in running the business can be exempted from management while still retaining their percentage of the profits. For instance, the owner of an LLC may decide to transfer the business to three members of his family. The person with the better business judgment can be appointed as manager of the company while the others simply earn a percentage of the profit without taking part in running the company.

8. Prestige: This is one of the little things that people seem to love about limited liability companies. The sound of "limited liability" seems a bit more prestigious than of "sole proprietor." For instance, which one do you think sounds more prestigious: "Acme Builders" or "Acme Builders, LCC"? The latter definitely sounds like a large, sophisticated company even though it is only a one-man operation that he runs out of his garage.

9. Separate Credit Rating: A Limited Liability Company is treated as a separate legal entity. This means that the company actually has its own credit rating independent of its owner's. This owner of an LLC can have a bad credit score, but this does not affect the company in any way.

Disadvantages of an LLC Compared to a Sole Proprietorship Business

Despite its advantages over a sole proprietorship or partnership, an LLC also has some disadvantages.

1. Cost: Operating a Limited Liability Company is slightly more expensive compared to a sole proprietorship or simple partnership. The startup cost is more similar to (or may even be slightly higher than) that of a corporation. A sole proprietorship business does not have to pay any annual fees or startup charges.

2. Taxes: Although a Limited Liability Company is more flexible in terms of taxation, it has some limitations as well. For instance, the owner of a Limited Liability Company may be required to pay unemployment compensation for himself. This is not necessary for a sole proprietorship.

3. Separate Records: Being a unique entity, the records of a Limited Liability Company must be kept separate from those of the owner. The owners of an LLC must keep their personal records apart from those of the company. Separate accounts must be maintained, and all monies received must be kept separate. This is both an advantage and a disadvantage. It means the owner or manager of the business has to go through extra stress to keep the records independent of each other.

LLCs Compared to Limited Partnerships

A limited partnership is a type of business entity owned by two groups of partners. One group (which can be one person or more) has control over the operations of the business. They are liable for the debts of the company. These are the general partners. The other group of partners only have investments in the company but do not participate in the management of the company. This means they are not liable for the debt of the business. These are referred to as limited partners.

Advantages of a Limited Liability Company Over a Limited Partnership

The main advantage of an LLC over a general partnership is that it provides liability protection for all the owners of the company. In a limited partnership, the general partners face the same liability concerns as a one-man business. Only the limited partners are free from this burden. An LLC offers equal protection for all members. Hence, there will be no need for general partners.

Additionally, an LLC also offers some unique tax advantages over a limited partnership. For example, it allows an increase in tax basis and passive losses. These provide the members with more deductions on their taxes. On the downside, the profits of a Limited Liability Company may still be subjected to Medicare taxes or social security taxes. These do not apply to a limited partnership.

Chapter Three: LLC Business Structures and Options

A Limited Liability Company is a very flexible business structure. This gives the owner(s) the freedom to configure the management and organization of the business as they deem fit. Some limited liability companies may be structured based on a specific professional service or organized in a way that takes advantage of some specific interstate commerce laws.

Types of LLCs

Although the legal structure of a Limited Liability Company is the same throughout the country, each state has unique rules governing its operation. Membership varies as well. An LLC may have just one member or several members. Here are the various types of limited liability companies.

Single-Member Limited Liability Company

Just like the name implies, a single-member LLC is owned by a single person. Hence, it is very similar to a sole proprietorship. The owner of the company is in charge of day to day company transactions. He is also responsible for doing the taxes and managing the company's debts. A single-member LLC may choose to be identified as a corporation or not. If the owner chooses not to be listed as a corporation, it will be classified as a "disregarded entity" under the law. In this case, the taxation is processed as a sole proprietorship. The single-member Limited Liability Company is the commonest type of Limited Liability Company. It is also the most affordable and requires less paperwork compared to other types.

General Partnership (Multiple Member LLC)

A Limited Liability Company can also be formed by multiple members. In this case, it will be referred to as a general partnership and all the members of the company will be in charge of the daily operation and transactions. They also take responsibility for the tax and debts of the business. Decision making in this kind of company is joint. Members have a say in when assets are purchased or sold. Each member will be required to pay taxes on their respective business income.

Family Limited Partnerships

This is the case when family members form a Limited Liability Company either as a single-member Limited Liability Company or as a general partnership. With a family limited partnership, members of the same families pool their assets to form the company. Hence, the family owns the business, but they can designate control to one member of the family.

Series LLC

This is a rare type of Limited Liability Company. In fact, only a few states in the US offer the option of a Series Limited Liability Company. A series LLC provides liability protection for members across multiple series. Each of these series is theoretically free from liabilities that may arise from the activities of other series. Each series are made up of business entities. The series may include members, managers, interests, and assets, each with their designated debts, rights, and obligations. Apart from Delaware, other states offering series LLC include Nevada, Illinois, Tennessee, Oklahoma, Iowa, Texas, and Utah. Each unit in the series LLC is taxed separately.

Restricted LLCs

The restricted Limited Liability Company is a new form of LLC that was introduced in 2009. Currently, it is only available in the state of Nevada. This form of Limited Liability Company is restricted by conditions in the articles of organization of the company. For instance, there is typically a ten-year waiting period before members of the LLC can start getting business distributions. This form of Limited Liability Company is also created under specific state rules in terms of the conditions for registration. These laws also set specific rules for the sales of the stock of such a company. There are also regulations that outline the voting power of shareholders, among other things.

The most significant feature of a restricted LLC is that the law allows a re-evaluation of the business worth based on a specific formula. This formula makes it possible to reduce the company's value based on new market value. This reduces the company's valuation discount. Consequently, the devalued company will pay lower taxes both at federal and state levels,

L3C Company

A low-profit Limited Liability Company is also known as an L3C. This type of LLC business entity is a bridge between non-profit and for-profit organizations. An L3C company provides a form of business structure that makes it possible for for-profit companies with socially beneficial programs to carry out charitable or social missions while still generating profits for its owners. An L3C company is typically established for philanthropic purposes, but the company also gets to enjoy the same tax benefits of conventional limited liability companies.

The main idea of this kind of business is to make it easy for companies to attract investment from charitable/philanthropic foundations and private investors. The Articles of Organization for forming for such a company and the tax requirement mirrors that of the traditional LLC system. This business structure is only available in a few U.S. states, namely Utah, Vermont, Louisiana, Rhode Island, Wyoming, and Maine.

Anonymous Limited Liability Company

An anonymous Limited Liability Company is just like any other regular Limited Liability Company. However, it offers an additional benefit of not disclosing the ownership information of the company to the public. This form of LLC is particularly desirable for companies who want to conduct their business with confidentiality.

Member-Managed LLC or Manager-Managed LLC

One of the core decisions in setting up an LLC is determining how the management will be structured. This and other details are usually specified in the operating agreement of the company. In terms of management, there are two main options. You can have a member-managed Limited Liability Company or a manager-managed LLC.

In the case of a member-managed Limited Liability Company, the day to day operation of the company is handled by the owners (members of the company). In this case, each of the members is authorized to act on behalf of the company. This is the more popular structure for the management of an LLC.

For a manager-managed LLC, an individual is appointed as a manager. He or she will be responsible for the daily operations of the company. The manager or managers will be specified in the company's operating agreement, with the consent of all the owners. Although the managers are usually appointed among the owners of the Limited Liability Company, they have rights and responsibilities different from that of the other owners. For example, the managers will have more voting rights, will be able to negotiate loans on behalf of the company, and handle operational tasks and financial affairs of the company. The non-managing owners of the company are free from all the obligations of operating the business.

The manager-managed approach is favored by companies with investors who typically prefer to remain as silent partners. This allows them to reap the reward of their investment without directly getting involved with the business. The fact that they are removed from the business also means they are less affected, and the business is more easily identified as a separate body when there are legal issues.

Domestic or Foreign LLC

A Limited Liability Company can also be domestic or foreign. This categorization is based on the state's laws under which the company is formed and where it operates. A Foreign Limited Liability Company is formed under the law of one state but does business in another state. In this case, the company will be subject to the laws of both states. However, the company will benefit from favorable tax laws and other laws in the state where it is formed. For instance, the state of Delaware is known for being quite favorable to businesses. You may choose to have your Limited Liability Company formed in Delaware despite operating in another state.

Key Considerations When Deciding Between a Single and Multi-Member LLC

1. Ownership: Although every state has their specific laws governing the creation of an LLC, the laws regarding ownership are quite similar in all states. Whether you are forming a single-member or multi-member LLC, ownership can include both citizens and non-citizens of the United States. Another corporation or LLC business may also form an LLC. As earlier explained, in the case of a single-member LLC, there is only one owner, and he or she has full control of the business. However, the LLC remains a legal entity on its own that is independent of the owner.

A Multi-member LLC, on the other hand, is owned by more than one member. They share control over the company. But the LLC is independent of its members. Members of the company may decide on how profit and losses will be shared among its members. The number of members that may form a multi-member LLC is unlimited. However, if you elect to have your LLC taxed as An S Corporation, the number of members cannot exceed 100.

The truth is, ownership is not a really important consideration in determining which type of LLC to form. Each of them have their own advantages and downsides. Some single business owners may find it more beneficial to switch to a multi-member LLC by simply making a spouse or relative a member. And in some cases, companies with multiple owners may opt for a single-member LLC. At the end of the day, it's all about individual preferences.

2. Management: A single-member limited liability company has only one owner who also acts as the manager of the business. In the case of a multi-member LLC, there are two options for managing the business. The members may opt for a member-managed system or a manager-managed system.

In the case of the member-managed business, all the members of the Limited Liability Company participate in managing the business. To make significant decisions like securing loans or entering a contract, there must be majority approval from all the members.

In the case of a manager-managed LLC business, the members appoint a member or members of the company to manage the business. A third party may also be appointed as a manager. The manager(s) has the authority to make decisions regarding the daily operation of the business. But the higher-level or strategic decisions of the company are still subject to the approval of all the members. But generally, they are only passive owners that only have financial interests in the company.

The member-managed system is the default arrangement recognized by state laws. If you want to form a manager-managed LLC, then it must be specified in the formation documents of the company. Regardless of the type of LLC that is being formed, the details must be specified in the operating agreement. This will ensure that all the members fully understand how the company will be operated. The operating agreement also includes the roles, responsibilities, and authority of each member. It also includes what happens if a member ends up leaving the company or dies.

3. Personal Asset Protection: There is really no difference in the level of personal asset protection offered by single-member and multi-member LLCs. No matter the management structure, the business remains a separate legal entity. Their personal properties are free from liabilities due to the activities of the business. In the event of legal disputes against the LLC, only the assets belonging to the company can be claimed. The members may lose their investment in the business, but nothing more.

However, there are situations where members may be held personally responsible for company issues. For instance, if a member participates in any illegal business activities or acts as a guarantor for a business loan for the company. In these cases, the personal properties of the member in question might be at risk.

3. Income Tax Treatment: A single-member Limited Liability Company is treated as a sole proprietorship in terms of federal taxes. Similarly, a multi-member company is treated as a partnership. The process of tax deductions is quite similar in either case. Unless the company elects to have it otherwise, the profits and losses of the business will be passed through to its owners. The owner of the business is expected to report this on the IRS Schedule C form 1040. The business will not have to pay any taxes as a separate entity. Additionally, the member(s) of the LLC will be required to pay self-employment taxes, which includes Medicare and social security taxes on all their taxable income from the business. These income taxes are estimated and paid quarterly. We will discuss how limited liability companies pay taxes in subsequent chapters of this book.

5. Compliance: Both single-member and multi-member limited liability companies have business compliance requirements. However, the process is generally less complex for a single-member LLC compared to multi-member LLCs. Following these compliance guidelines is important to maintain the personal liability protection that the members enjoy. Some of the tasks they need to follow include:

- Paying taxes and other fees
- Holding annual meetings, keeping minutes, and submitting annual reports
- Renewing licenses and permits
- Maintaining company records

There may also be additional compliance requirements depending on the state where the business operates. An LLC that violates these requirements may be fined, penalized, or have their business suspended. As expected, keeping up with these requirements is easier for a one-man Limited Liability Company since it is essentially a much smaller company compared to a multi-member company.

These are the major considerations that may influence your decision to form a multi-member or a single-member LLC. You can make a more informed decision by consulting with your attorney or trusted business advisor.

Chapter Four: LLC Taxes Explained

A Limited Liability Company is typically not recognized by the IRS as a business entity for taxation purposes. So, if you register your company as an LLC, how exactly will you pay your taxes?

According to the IRS, a multi-member Limited Liability Company may be treated as a partnership or corporation for the purpose of taxation. It may also be "disregarded" as a legal entity and treated independently of its owner if it is a one-member LLC.

So essentially, the way an LLC will pay taxes depends on whether it is registered as a single-member or multiple-member LLC. It also depends on if the LLC has elected to be treated as a separate taxable entity or not.

How does a single-member Limited Liability Company pay tax?

A single-member Limited Liability Company will be taxed like any sole proprietorship business. This type of business is treated as a disregarded entity. Basically, what this means is that the LLC and its owner(s) are considered separate entities. The owner, rather than the company, is taxed.

The implication of this is that all the company's profit and loss information will be filled into a Schedule C form. The net income calculated from this form will be brought into line twelve of the personal tax return for the business owner. This system is the default way of filing taxes for a one-member LLC.

How do multiple-member limited liability companies pay their income taxes?

Since a multiple-member LLC will have two or more members, the method used to prepare the income tax of this type of company is more similar to that of a partnership. Partnership businesses, like sole proprietorships, are not required to pay taxes to the IRS. Instead, each partner is required to pay their respective taxes based on their individual share of the company's profits.

The business is expected to file information returns using IRS form 1065. Subsequently, each member of the business will prepare a Schedule K-1 form. The gain or loss will be indicated on each member's 1040 form. Unless indicated otherwise, the IRS treats the taxation of any registered LLC this way. However, both single and multiple-member LLCs may elect to be classified as a corporation or as a pass-through business.

How income tax is filed for Limited liability companies classified as S corporations:

An LLC may choose to be treated as an S corporation only for taxation purposes. There are specific advantages of having your business classified this way. It is particularly favorable for businesses where the individual earns a higher income because they get to pay lower taxes.

An LLC company that opts to operate as an S corporation will follow these tax laws at the federal level and also pay state income tax. But the income of individual members is not taxed. The company will continue its operation as a Limited Liability Company in every other respect.

How do Limited Liability Companies that operate as pass-through businesses pay tax?

Limited Liability Companies that elect not to pay taxes as an S Corporations are referred to as pass-through businesses. This means that the business tax will be passed through to members of the company. It will be included as part of the income tax return for each individual, after each has received their share of the net income, based on the company's operating agreement.

For instance, consider a Limited Liability Company with 2 owners who share their profits equally. If the net profit of their business is $100,000, which is shared equally between them, then each owner will pay income tax on his or her share of $50,000. The income and loss from their Limited Liability Company will be considered together with the other incomes of the member from other businesses. This is their total tax liability. The profits from the Limited Liability Company will be considered as self-employment tax liability. However, if the company makes no profit within the tax period, then the member does not owe self-employment tax for that period.

Since tax flexibility is one of the major reasons most people create a Limited Liability Company, you should understand how LLC taxes are filed. This and other processes involved in running a Limited Liability Company will be covered in the next chapter.

PART TWO: Forming Your LLC

Chapter Five: Starting from Scratch or Converting?

Many small businesses start off either as a sole proprietorship or partnership. However, there might come a time when you, as a business owner, will need to legally expand the structure of your small business.

This decision can be due to different reasons. You might have noticed that your small business is getting bigger, and you are realizing that personal assets are at risk if your business were to be sued or go into debt.

In setting up a Limited Liability Company, there are two main options. For businesses just starting out with no prior registration, you need to follow the process of forming your LLC from scratch. It is also possible that corporations that have been in business for some years decide to convert to an LLC. In this case, you have the option of statutory conversion, statutory merger, or non-statutory conversion. This chapter will cover the process of forming an LLC, depending on which of these routes you are taking. We begin with how to form a Limited Liability Company from scratch.

Forming an LLC from Scratch – An Overview

Forming a limited liability from scratch is the same no matter the type of LLC you decide to create. There are only a few slight differences, depending on state regulations and other minor factors. We will cover this process in greater detail in this section. But first, here is a simple overview of the overall process of forming an LLC from scratch.

1. Choosing a Business Name: Like every business, one of the fundamental steps in forming an LLC is choosing a business name. You will need to search and verify if the name you have chosen is still available.

2. Apply for an Employer Identification Number (EIN): All limited liability companies are required to have an EIN. This is compulsory, whether you have hired employees yet or not. The EIN is issued for free by the IRS.

3. Designate a Registration Agent: All LLCs are required to appoint a registered agent. The registration agent will be in charge of receiving legal documents and notices from the IRS and other government bodies. The registered agent must have a physical residential address in the state where the business is registered.

4. File Articles of Organization with the State: This is the next crucial step in the process of creating an LLC. You will need to pay the filing fee and get the necessary document(s) in the State where the business is registered or in which it operates. The fees and information required may vary from state to state.

5. Complete Entity Classification Election Form: The next crucial step is to complete the IRS Form 8832. This form will determine the tax status of the LLC. A Limited Liability Company may opt to be taxed as a corporation or like a sole proprietorship business.

6. Creating an Operating Agreement: This is a set of documents that includes critical rules on how the LLC will operate. It is not a document required by states for registration, but this document is vital for running an LLC. It will govern issues like how the authority will be designated among members, profit distribution, and dispute management, among other details. Even single-member limited liability companies need an operating agreement since the document helps to support the company's limited liability status.

7. Opening a Bank Account for your Business: Like a corporation, an LLC requires a dedicated bank account. This is an important step that helps to maintain the corporate veil of the business, ensuring the protection of the company members.

8. Obtaining Permits and Licenses: Aside from registering your business with the IRS and other relevant bodies, you also need to obtain special licenses and permits. This will allow you to conduct your business legally. The process for this depends on the type of business you operate and your location.

9. Learn the Employment and Hiring Requirement Laws: If your Limited Liability Company hires employees, then you must be familiar with various employment rules and abide by them. You may also be required to submit reports to the state, federal, or local government periodically.

This is a quick overview of all the steps you will need to follow to set up your Limited Liability Company. We will go into this in greater detail in subsequent chapters of this book.

In addition to all of these, you will also need information about the daily running of your business. One of such issues is taxation. Staying tax-compliant is important to maintain the corporate status of your LLC. In the next chapter, I will give a brief overview of LLC taxes. This will be discussed in greater detail in subsequent chapters.

Converting your Current Company to a Limited Liability Company

The alternative method for setting up a Limited Liability Company is to convert an existing business into an LLC. Typically, this process involves converting an already registered corporation into an LLC. However, know that this is not an entirely straightforward process. Multiple factors can influence how this entire process goes, and can give rise to a wide range of scenarios. Some of the variable factors in the process of forming an LLC from an already existent company include:

- **The Type of Corporation**: As earlier explained in this book, there are two kinds of corporations: S schedule corporations and C corporations. C Corporations pay corporate taxes. S corporations, on the other hand, do not pay corporate taxes; instead, the shareholders are taxed through a pass-through taxation system.

- **State Regulations:** Corporations are allowed to be formed under one state's laws while operating in another state. This factor may be significant in the conversion process.

- **Type of LLC to be Formed:** Another factor that may affect the conversion process is the end product. Do you want your corporation to be converted to a single-member LLC or a multi-member LLC?

- **Taxation:** Taxation is usually one of the major motivations for converting a corporation into an LLC. It is only normal that it is an important consideration for forming your company. The newly formed LLC may be taxed as a partnership or a corporation or as a disregarded entity.

- **Method of Conversion:** Corporations can be converted to limited liability companies through statutory conversion, statutory merger, or non-statutory conversion.

As you can see, these variables will influence the conversion process one way or another. For instance, if you use the statutory merger method to convert an already existing C Corporation to a Limited Liability Company, so it can be taxed as a partnership, the process and paperwork will be different than that of the statutory conversion method to convert an S corporation to an LLC that will be taxed as a corporation.

The truth is, we cannot possibly cover every likely scenario that may arise here. But I will try to give a somewhat general overview of what this conversion process may entail. I'll try to simplify the process as much as possible. I will use one of the most common scenarios (converting a C corporation to a multi-member LLC) to explain the three methods of converting your company to an LLC.

Statutory Conversion

This is a relatively new procedure for converting an existing company into an LLC. This is a more streamlined and simpler process. However, it is not available in all states yet. Under this method, you can convert a corporation to an LLC by simply filing some forms at the office of the Secretary of State in the state where your company is registered. However, the process varies from state to state, and some states do not permit this process of conversion at all.

With this method, you can complete the process of converting your company in four simple steps:

• The directors of the corporation have to meet and approve the conversion.

• The directors create a plan for conversion then recommend the plan to the stakeholders who have to approve it.

• The conversion plan is put to a vote by the stakeholder. A majority vote is needed to proceed with the process.

• The directors can then proceed to file a certificate of conversion. The LLC certificate of formation and other needed documentation will also be filed with the office of the Secretary of State.

The implications of this process are straightforward. Once the statutory conversion process has been completed, the corporate stakeholders in the corporation become members of the newly formed LLC. This process is also quite straightforward in terms of asset transfer, and this is one of its advantages over other methods. The assets and liabilities of the corporation will be automatically transferred to the new LLC, as the old corporation no longer exists. With statutory conversion, all the processes are wrapped up into one. There is no need to set up a separate agreement for transferring stocks of members or their assets. No additional legal filings are required. Hence, the statutory conversion is not only faster but also cheaper than the other methods of conversion. If this is available in your state, then it is the most recommended option.

Statutory Merger

This one is a bit more complicated compared to the statutory conversion method. However, this is the next best thing, especially if your business is located in a state that does not have the option of statutory conversion available. Each state has its specific rules governing the process of the statutory merger, but the general process is essentially the same:

- A new Limited Liability Company is formed with the stakeholders in the corporation as members of the new Limited Liability Company.
- The stakeholders of the corporation must vote for a merger of their roles as members of the new LLC and stakeholders of the corporation.
- The stakeholders have to initiate a process that formally exchanges their shares for membership rights in the LLC.
- They must also file for a merger certificate and other legal documents from the office of the Secretary of State.

Just like the statutory conversion method, this method also legally transfers the liabilities and assets of the corporation to the newly formed LLC. However, before this transfer can take place, the new LLC must be formed as a separate entity first. This process involves several steps and additional fees. This makes the process of statutory merger more time consuming and expensive. Stakeholders also have to formally move to have their corporate shares changed to membership rights through the merger agreement (a process not needed in the case of statutory conversion). Many states also require the stakeholders to file for the dissolution of the corporation once the merger has been completed.

Non-Statutory Conversion

This is the most complex of the three methods of converting a corporation to an LLC. It is also a more expensive process, since there are a lot of steps involved. The steps involved include:

- Formation of a new Limited Liability Company
- The formal transfer of the assets & liabilities of the corporation to the LLC
- The formal exchange of stakeholder shares for membership rights in the newly formed LLC.
- Formal liquidation and dissolution of the corporation.

Unlike the other conversion methods, the non-statutory method of conversion does not automatically transfer the assets and liabilities of the corporation to the newly formed LLC. Instead, after forming the LLC, special agreements will have to be formulated to transfer these liabilities and assets. Additionally, special agreements will also be needed for the conversion of corporate shares to membership interests in the new company. Because the non-statutory conversion method tends to be more complicated, you may need legal assistance to get it done. Unless it is the only option available, this is not a recommended approach.

Before you go through the process of converting your corporation to an LLC, be sure to check the conversion and merger laws in your state. These tend to vary from state to state. For example, in California there is a conversion statute that makes it possible for corporations in the state to switch to an LLC structure by completing a form known as the LLC-1A. This form helps to simplify the process and skips some of the steps that are compulsory under the statutory merger or non-statutory conversion method. The state of Arizona has no conversion statue at all. Although corporations are allowed to merge into an LLC, they cannot simply change to a Limited Liability Company. This means the only options you get for converting your corporation into an LLC in Arizona are statutory merger and non-statutory conversion.

Important Tax Considerations for Conversion to an LLC

Perhaps the most complicated part of converting a corporation to a Limited Liability Company is working out the taxation rules for the new company. You must have this figured out before making the conversion since taxation is one of the major differences between the different types of business structures.

For example, if you convert from a C corporation to an LLC that elects to be taxed like a partnership, this will result in a larger tax bill. The corporation will be taxed along with the liquidation (transfer or sale) of its asset. The shareholders will also be taxed on any asset that is distributed among them. This will result in double taxation. Despite any factors that may affect the taxes, it is unlikely that any of the potential benefits of this conversion outweigh the cost of taxation.

If you are switching from a corporation to a Limited Liability Company that will still be taxed as a corporation, the adverse tax effects are a lot less than the scenario earlier described. The IRS can consider this conversion in either of these two ways:

- A straight exchange of stakeholder shares for LLC membership, which falls under IRC (internal revenue code) section 1036.
- An "F reorganization" that is largely tax-free.

However, although the tax bill is lower, the details of how the bill will be calculated may not be that straightforward, especially if it is treated as an F reorganization. Similarly, no matter how the IRS bills the taxation for the conversion, it does not affect how the business will pay taxes later on as an LLC. Hence, you must thoroughly investigate how this type of conversion will affect your company in terms of taxation.

You may also choose to convert your C Corporation to a Limited Liability Company that will be treated as a disregarded entity by the IRS. This is usually the case if you are converting a corporation to a single-member LLC or subsidiary of a larger corporation into a

Limited Liability Company. This system also applies if you are merging a corporation into a disregarded-entity that will be wholly owned by another corporation.

Each of these conversion options has its consequences as far as taxes are concerned. In the case of a single-owner LLC, for example, the conversion will be treated as if the old corporation is being liquidated, and associated taxes will be charged.

The examples treated so far refer specifically to conversion from a C corporation to a Limited Liability Company. The rules are slightly different for conversion that involve S corporations, especially in terms of taxation. An S corporation operates on a single level of taxation. The corporation itself is not taxed, but the shareholders have to pay taxes. Hence, the tax consequences of the conversion are limited compared to when a C corporation is involved. However, this advantage only applies to the conversion itself. Since both Limited liability companies and S corporations operate on a pass-through taxation basis, one has to wonder what advantages a business will gain from making such a conversion in the first place.

As you can see, the process of converting an existing business to a Limited Liability Company can be quite elaborate and complicated. You will also need an in-depth knowledge of the taxation rules involved both for the conversion itself and on the new LLC business when the conversion is complete. All these are important factors that must be carefully weighed before initiating the conversion process.

Chapter Six: Naming Your Company

The first and perhaps the most important step of creating a Limited Liability Company is choosing a business name. Not only important for the subsequent registration of your business and creating the articles of organization, a business name also serves legal and marketing purposes. Hence, choosing the right one is important. You want a business name that stands out and does a good job of communicating the products or services your business offers to people. You also want a name that is memorable, and easy to pronounce. But above all, your business name must meet all the legal naming requirements of a Limited Liability Company in your state of registration.

Considering all the many facets of choosing a business name, it is definitely worth spending your time and effort on the right name. Even though changing the name of your LLC later is quite possible, it will be best if you can get it right the first time. You don't want to waste all the brand recognition you have gained on a previous name when you have to change it in the future. Your LLC business name is something that you will hopefully use for a while, so putting in all the work now to get it right is not a bad idea.

So how do you go about choosing an LLC name? I will cover the most important considerations for choosing the right name for your company.

Brainstorm

The first thing to do is to brainstorm name ideas and produce a list of possible names. You can draw inspiration from your idea or concept of your business or personal sentiments. However, you cannot simply pick a great name out of thin air. You need to be creative with the process. Still, your creativity will best serve you when you put some helpful restrictions in place. You can produce a list of four to five names and choose the most fitting one based on the following considerations.

Is it legal?

Arguably the most important consideration in choosing a name for your Limited Liability Company is to ensure that it is legal. This will require you to be familiar with the list of required words that must be included and restricted words to be avoided in an LLC business name.

Adding a Limited Liability Company designation to your company is compulsory in almost every state. You can include the phrase "Limited Liability Company" or any other variation like "limited liability," "LLC," or "L.L.C" in the company name. For example, John & Sons LLC or Betty Lane Limited Liability Company. This is the only identifier that is made compulsory in all states.

States also have rules about words that *cannot* be included in the name of a Limited Liability Company. There are also restricted words that can only be used only in special conditions or with permission. For instance, words like "insurance" or "bank" are restricted words in most states. Some words are restricted to the naming of professional limited liability companies, and the process of registering such companies is different from regular LLCs. You should be able to find a list of restricted words or phrases for an LLC business name on the website of the Secretary of State in your state of registration. Be sure to include this in your consideration and strike out words or phrases that are non-compliant.

Branding Considerations for Choosing an LLC Name

Your Limited Liability Company is a brand offering a product for sale or selling a service. Therefore, you have to consider the branding implication of whatever name you finally settle on. You can find loads of material online that deal specifically with the subject of branding your business. However, here are some major considerations for branding your Limited Liability Company.

Make the Name Memorable

You want the name of your company to be one that people can easily remember. Whether you are using a play on words or an alliteration, choosing a memorable name will make it easier to keep your business in their minds. You don't want a potential customer or client to have trouble remembering the name of your business the next time they need your service or want to recommend your business to someone.

It is best to avoid acronyms and simply use names directly. It will cost you more in terms of marketing if you try to grab people's attention with a few letters. However, if you intend to shorten your business name, you can condense a longer name into an amalgam. For instance, Nabisco is the amalgam for the National Biscuit Company, while FedEx stands for Federal Express.

Longer names are often are usually more memorable than shorter names. So, you don't have to restrain yourself with the length of the name. You are also more likely to be able to find a unique domain name with a longer name than a short one.

Be Expansive & Global

One common mistake business owners make with naming is choosing a name that restrains their business to one location or niche. Unless you intend to create other versions of your business in other places, the name "Los Angeles Rentals" sounds pretty restrictive. You will have to rebrand or create a separate business if you decide to expand into other states in the future. Also, while choosing a niche is helpful, it is best to avoid tagging your name as specific to your business niche. That way, you will not be restricted if you decide to move your business forward. Unless, of course, your niche is a large one, and you have no plans whatsoever to expand into other areas in the future.

You should also try to make your business name internationally friendly. It would be bad to find out that your business name has a negative connotation in other cultures when you decide to expand your business abroad. For example, there is a brand of Toyota minivan with the name "Previa." Although this means "preview" in Spanish and Italian, in English, the words placenta previa refer to a condition where a baby's birth is obstructed by the placenta. Not a good name for a car, if you ask me!

Be Eternal

Some names sounded fashionable years ago but will sound completely outrageous today. Since most LLCs have a perpetual existence, try to choose a name that will sound good for many decades or centuries down the road. For instance, how does Twentieth Century Fox sound to you now that we're in the 21st century?

Make It Meaningful

You should choose a name that gives people an idea of what you are selling or the services you are offering. For example, the name "Jake and Dolly's Fascinating Whatzits" gives no clue whatsoever about what the company is selling. Being able to choose a name that gives people an idea of what to expect from your business is invaluable.

Careful here, though! When I say choose a meaningful name, I don't mean you have to give everything about your business away in its name. That is what tag lines and slogans are for. For example, choose between "Netflix" and "MoviesOnline" as business names. The winner is obvious, isn't it? You still get a hint of what Netflix means, but

MoviesOnline is a little too descriptive. Just make your company name as evocative as much as possible without giving out too much.

Be Original

The need for originality cannot be overemphasized. Although traditional trademark laws allow two firms to have similar names, newly introduced "anti-dilution laws" introduce some new challenges that you don't want to deal with. These laws make it possible for companies with "famous trademarks" to stop others from trying to do business with rip-offs of their name. So, while it may seem like a good idea to have a name that makes you sound like the big boys, you must steer clear of names that are already in use. Plus, you don't want your business sounding like a cheap rip-off when it really isn't.

The need for originality is even more important for internet-based businesses where you need originality to stand out from the competition. If your business name sounds too similar to another domain name, some of your traffic may end up going to that website.

Before you settle on a name, you should try to search for it to see what pops up. If there are too many results showing businesses with the same or similar names, you should change the name even if these businesses are not in the same physical location or serve the same niche as yours.

Generally, most states don't permit businesses to choose names that are confusingly similar to other businesses registered in the same state. In most cases, the state agency in charge of registration may offer a searchable online database of registered businesses in the state. You can use this database to conduct an LLC name search to confirm if the name you intend to choose is still available.

Marketing Considerations for Naming for your LLC

If your business name is not marketable, selling your product or service is most likely going to be difficult. There are several strategies that you will need to use to market your business. But if you choose an unfavorable business name, it will be difficult to make people recognize your brand and buy your products or services. Hence, before you choose an LLC name, think of the impact of the name on your marketing efforts.

Most marketing plans involve letting potential customers know about the services you offer. Think of how helpful choosing a name that aligns with the core values of your business will be. Try to tie one or two words together that are related to what you do or how you do business. This is a great creative standpoint from which to start thinking of your business name while keeping marketing in mind.

Keep it Simple

I know I mentioned earlier that longer names are more memorable. Still, a name that is too complex will hurt your marketing efforts. Keep the name short, simple, and easy to pronounce. You don't want people wondering if your business name is pronounced one way or another. If there is a simpler version of the name you have in mind, use it!

Make It Domain-Name Friendly

In this Internet-fueled era, choosing a name that is internet friendly is everything. Even if your business is not internet-based, you still need some form of online presence, usually in the form of a website. To set up a website, you need to choose a domain name. Even if you are not setting up a website immediately, check the business name register to see if the domain name associated with your business (or a very close variant of it) is still available. There is nothing worse than discovering there is no possible domain name available for your business after settling on a perfect name.

Also, some names may look good on paper, but terrible as a domain name. Take, for example, the name "Choose Spain"; it does not sound as bad as the name of a company selling lovely products from Spain. But when it is mashed together in a domain name like "choosespain.net," it doesn't look so good anymore. Since your website will most likely be the core of your marketing efforts, this is an important consideration.

Make It Social Media Friendly

Social media is another essential component of business marketing these days. Choosing a name that you can easily promote on social media is important. Just like the domain name search, you should check the major social media platforms like Facebook, Twitter, Instagram, and Pinterest for the availability (or close variants) of the name you intend to pick.

By putting all of these together, you should be able to come up with a great name for your business that not only meets the legal criteria but also sells your product and services effectively. Remember, that the LLC name isn't merely a means of identifying your business; your branding, and marketing efforts will be built on it as well. So, try to get it right and choose a name that is worth its weight in gold.

Chapter Seven: Creating Your Articles of Organization

Now that you have a cool and unique name picked out for your company, it's time to set the ball rolling and get down to the details of establishing your Limited Liability Company. Several steps have to be completed before you can achieve this, beginning with the creation of your articles of organization. Now, that probably sounds like some legal mumbo-jumbo. But creating your articles of organization is the most important step in the process of creating your Limited Liability Company. So, what exactly are the articles of organization?

What are the Articles of Organization?

The articles of organization of a Limited Liability Company are documents that act as a charter for the existence of a Limited Liability Company in any U.S. state. The articles also include some basic information about the newly formed LLC.

The articles of organization are filed together as a single document with the office of the Secretary of State or any state agency that is in charge of business registration. Basically, this document describes the basic operating characteristics and identifying details of the Limited Liability Company. Filling this document and its consequent approval by the relevant state authority legally creates the LLC and seals its status as a registered company within that state.

An article of an organization is the legal document that creates an LLC. It is equivalent to the certificate of incorporation or articles of incorporation that you will need to file when you are forming a corporation. The Articles of an organization is a basic requirement for the formation of an LLC in all US states. However, it may be called other names in different states. For instance, states like Washington, Texas, New Hampshire, Mississippi, Maine, Delaware, and Alabama refer to it as the Certificate of Formation. It is called the Certificate of Organization in Utah, Pennsylvania, Massachusetts, Iowa, Idaho, and Connecticut.

The Process of Filing LLC Organizing Documents

Aside from the difference in name across various states, the information required for the creation of the articles of organization may also vary from one state to another. In this next section, we will go over, step-by-step, the process of creating the Articles of Organization for a Limited Liability Company. Note that there might be slight variations in your home state, but the general process highlighted here pretty much sums it up.

Step One: Check Secretary-of-State Website for your State

The first step in creating the articles of organization is to visit the website for the secretary of state or the relevant agency in charge of business registration in your specific state. Here, you will find all the information you need to create the articles of organization and all the items you need to include in your application. You should also find a detailed guide that works you through the process. Check to see if this form is available online or if you have to visit a physical location to file it. Typically, the filing cost for your articles of organization may be anywhere between $50 and $200. How much you will be charged also depends on your state.

Step Two: Gather the Information You Need for Filing

Before you proceed to fill out the form, there is some basic information you will be required to provide. It is best to collect all of this information beforehand. This will include information on the company itself as well as its owners.

Name of the Limited Liability Company: In the previous chapter, we already went over the process of picking a name for your company and important considerations for picking the right name. That stage of the process must be completed first before you can proceed to create articles of organization.

Once you have settled on a name, you are expected to carry out a business entity search to ensure its uniqueness. The name you put in your articles of organization is expected to include a "Limited Liability Company" designation or just "LLC." Some states do not allow the inclusion of certain words in an LLC business name. Words like "bank", "insurance", or "trust" cannot be included in an LLC name in many states.

Principal Place of Business: You will need to include the main location or headquarters of your company in the application form. The principal place of business is simply an address where the management of the company works or where company records are kept. The street address, not just the P.O. box, will be required for this. If you run the business from home, you can put down your home address as the principal place of business. In this case, your business will get a home-office tax deduction.

The Registered Agent: This is a requirement for the registration of an LLC (and pretty much all forms of business entities) in every US state. A registered agent is someone who sends and receives official paperwork on behalf of your business. He or she receives important legal documents from both state and federal agencies. A registered agent is also in charge of receiving service of process documents for your business. This includes legal documents like subpoenas or summons or any other form of notifications relating to a lawsuit. Registered agents are also known as statutory agents or agents of process. You may appoint an attorney, a corporate director, or a CPA to act as your registered agent. Some third-party agents perform this duty.

Although there is no rule that says you cannot act as your own registered agent, this is not common practice. Neither is it something I would recommend. A registered agent must be an individual that is available in one location to receive correspondence. It is unlikely that you will want to add this to the stress of running your company, which is why designating the duty to someone else is recommended.

The name and address of your designated registered agent will be included in your articles of organization as well as other public records. A simple search online should turn up some registered agents within your state.

Dates: another detail you will have to include on your Articles of Organization is the official launch date of your LLC. However, if there is no specific start date yet, you can simply use the date when the application was filed and accepted. Your state may also have specific rules about the date. You should check for this as well.

If the Limited Liability Company is expected to have a lifespan, then you can also state the specific duration through which the company is expected to last. However, since most LLCs last perpetually, most states do not make providing this information compulsory.

Organizational and Operational Details of your LLC: You will also be required to answer questions regarding the organization and operation of your LLC. Some of the details you may be required to provide include:

The Name of the Organizer: The organizer of a Limited Liability Company is someone that acts in order to form that LLC. This may be the owner(s) of the company or someone else.

Provide Professional Details: This is applicable for limited liability companies that will be providing a specific professional service. Such companies will have to specify this in the articles of organization. Businesses affected include those offering services like dentistry, chiropractic, law, medicine, public accounting, veterinary medicine, and psychology, among others.

Purpose: In some cases, you may be required to describe the purpose of the Limited Liability Company you want to form. The rules regarding this vary from state to state. For instance, in the State of Florida, LLCs that will be offering professional services must clearly state this in their statement of purpose. It should be written as "the practice of accounting, law, medicine...and so on," as the case may be. However, most states do not require a specific statement of purpose. Instead, a more general statement will be acceptable. For example, it may be written as "to engage in any lawful business for profit."

Management of the LLC: Another vital piece of information that must be included in the articles of organization is the LLC management details. We have already covered the two types of management structures of LLCs. You need to decide if the company will be member-managed or a manager will be appointed. Most states only require you to state which management format will be used, but some states may also require you to name specifically the manager designated for the business. Most limited liability companies are member-managed, which means everyone takes part in running the business. Some state laws will ask you to include the names and addresses of all the initial members of the LLC in the article of organization form.

Once you have filled in all the details above and completed the form accordingly, it should be signed by the authorized representative of the business. You can either mail the completed form along with the check for payment as specified on the website or submit it electronically. The procedure for submission should be specified on the Secretary of State website.

Additional information about creating the articles of organization:

As mentioned, most states require you to include a "Limited Liability Company" or "LLC" designation along with the name of the company. This is a compulsory requirement in most states. Since you are creating an LLC and not a corporation, do not use the term "Incorporated" or "Inc." for your Limited Liability Company.

Once you have completed the process of creating your articles of organization, there is no need to register the name of your business separately. The filing of the articles of organization is equivalent to registering your business name.

Although this is not a rule, you should use an official business checking account for the check. This will make your business look more legitimate. Although some banks will not allow you to create an account for your business until the articles of organization have been filed, most banks will.

You should keep a copy of the application form, whether in printed form or electronically, so you don't have to re-create it if it is needed in the future. In some states, you may be required to publish the articles of organization. For instance, in New York, a newly formed Limited Liability Company is required to publish a copy of the articles of organization or a notice of the formation of the company in two newspapers within 120 days of the approval of the articles.

Do You Need an Attorney for creating the Articles of Organization?

This is a matter of choice; there is really no rule concerning this. You can choose to complete the articles of the organization all by yourself or hire an attorney to complete the process for you. However, each state has its own rules for certain sections of the articles of organization. The process is best handled by someone who is more familiar with the rules and understands the process better.

What Next?

The articles of the organization officially create your Limited Liability Company. However, there are still some things that you have to check off your list before your company can begin operation. They may not be compulsory, but they are absolutely necessary for the smooth operation of your LLC.

Create an Operating Agreement

The operating agreement is similar to the by-laws of a corporation. This is a set of conditions that regulates the activities and operations of your limited liability company. It states how the business will be managed, how assets will be used, and how the revenues of the business will be shared among members. The operating agreement also specifies the rights and responsibilities of each member of the LLC. Some states have some default rules in the articles of organization, which may not be favorable to your business. The operating agreement effectively overrides these rules by describing exactly how your LLC will be operated. Hence, creating this agreement is quite important. In the next chapter, I will go explain the process of creating an operating agreement in greater detail.

Check the Annual Registration Requirements

To keep your business active, most states will require you to send in an annual or biennial report and pay a registration fee. You should look for the specific requirements for this process with your state authority. The purpose of this annual registration is to maintain an active status for your LLC and to provide current information about the management structure, business address, and other information about your LLC.

Obtain LLC Status in Other States

Although this is not compulsory, you can obtain an LLC status in other states outside your home state. This offers your company the same liability protection you enjoy in your home state in another state as well. It also makes your business look a lot more professional, which is quite attractive to prospective investors.

Run a Press Release

Once your LLC status has been approved, you may choose to run a press release in a local newspaper to announce the good news. This is a great way to attract attention to your business, draw in new clients, and get the attention of local investors who may be interested in your business.

Get an Employee Identification Number (EIN)

Even if you have yet to hire an employee for your business, you should get an Employee identification number. An EIN is compulsory if you intend to hire employees. Also, you can easily give your EIN to vendors or anyone else that needs it instead of giving out your social security number.

Obtain a Business Credit Card

If you do not have one already, I strongly recommend that you create a business bank account and get a business ID card to go with it. A business credit card will make it possible to track your purchases. This is especially important if you have employees or members that will have authority to purchase. This piece of documentation may also come in handy in case of litigation.

Acquire Business Insurance

While a Limited Liability Company provides personal protection for you against personal suits, getting business insurance will protect your business directly. If you can afford it, I recommend getting business insurance to cover potential damages, losses, or claims. Like all forms of insurance, getting business insurance will cost you. But in the long run, this may turn out to be less than the cost of not having it.

Chapter Eight: The LLC Operating Agreement

The Limited Liability Company operating agreement is a document that makes it possible to define the structure as well as the financial and working relationships of the co-owners (members) of a newly formed Limited Liability Company. It is the working document in which the operating guidelines of the LLC are stated. The operating agreement is the LLC equivalent of the articles of incorporation which govern the operation of a newly formed corporation.

Some of the details that must be included in the operating agreement include the company's statement of intent, the purpose of the business, the duration of the company's lifetime, and so on.

The operating agreement will also contain information about the membership of the business, their rights, and their responsibilities. Some of the membership details include the capital contributions of each member and their resultant share of the profit. It also itemizes how much control each person gets, how new members can join, and what happens in the event of the exit of a member.

As you can see, the operating agreement is a pretty detailed document. But is it compulsory to have one? Here are some of the reasons why you need to have an operating agreement for your Limited Liability Company.

Why You Need an Operating Agreement

In most states, an operating agreement is not a legal requirement for the creation of a Limited Liability Company. However, it would be quite unethical and unwise to try to run your Limited Liability Company without an operating agreement. While the details included in an operating agreement seem to be more relevant to a multi-member Limited Liability Company, you need to create one even if you are the sole owner of your LLC. This is because the operating agreement is pivotal to the maintenance of your company's limited liability status. In case of litigation, any form of mismanagement, or financial misunderstanding, you can refer to this document. It offers protection for members of the LLC against any personal liability.

While it may not seem like it, a sole proprietorship LLC needs an operating agreement just as much as a multiple-member company. Without the formality of this written agreement, your LLC is still very much like a sole proprietorship. The operating agreement will bring credence to the separate existence of your company as an entity before the law. This is the primary purpose of the operating agreement.

Other reasons why you may need an operating agreement include:

To Define the Management and Financial Structure of your LLC

This point is particularly relevant to LLCs owned by multiple members. The only document that contains the decision-making protocols and the profit-sharing plan for your LLC is an operating agreement. Without it, the co-owners of the company will not understand how the profits from the business will be shared and how management will be organized. This document also contains details of the process of admitting new members and how the departure of an existing member will be handled. These are issues that may cause problems between members of the company if the background rules are not properly set.

Overriding State Default Rules

Usually, every state will have laws governing the basic operation of a Limited Liability Company. These laws will most likely be included as default in the articles of organization (see the previous chapter). Although these default laws are not compulsory, the only valid way to override them is through the operating agreement, which allows you to set new rules upon which your company will operate.

For instance, in many states, the default rule for profit-sharing in a Limited Liability Company is for the profit to be shared equally among all members. This is not always practical. In many limited liability companies, investment sharing is based on the investment of each individual member in the business. As long as the co-owners did not invest an equal amount in the company, profit cannot be allocated equally.

However, without the operating agreement, the default rules stand. To override this default rule and others, you need to clearly indicate the terms of operation of your LLC in the operating agreement. The operating agreement makes it possible to set up your own rules and spell out the details of the inner workings of your Limited Liability Company. But what does this document contain, and how do you prepare one?

What to Include in Your Operating Agreement

An operating agreement is a highly detailed document that covers a whole range of issues regarding your Limited Liability Company. Most of these details are unique to your company, so you can't simply copy another LLC's operating agreement. Some of the details will depend on the specific situation of your company and the relationship between the business owners. Some of the most basic details that will be spelled out in an operating agreement include:

- The percentage of interest of each member in the LLC
- The rights and responsibilities of the owners
- Their voting power or authority on decision making
- Allocation of business profits and loss
- Management of the company
- Rules for meetings, note-taking, and decision making
- Management of cases of sale and purchase of interests and what happens upon the exit

of a member.

It is expected that the operating agreement covers these major areas. Although all of these may seem simple and straightforward, they are major decisions regarding the company. There will be a need for rigorous and continuous coordination with members to reach consensus and spell out the terms of this agreement.

Basic Provisions of the Operating Agreement of a Limited Liability Company

While an operating agreement typically contains several important details, some basic provisions must be included. Any operating agreement for a Limited Liability Company (whether single or multiple-member) is expected to include these basic details:

Identifying Information

The operating agreement is expected to clearly identify the LLC. The identifying information includes the Limited Liability Company's registered name, the address of the registered office, and the business's principal operating officer.

The Statement of Intent

This statement indicates that the operating agreement is in accordance with the limited liability laws of the state. This statement also confirms that the business will come into existence when the official LLC documentation has been filed with the state authorities.

Statement of Business Purpose

This states the purpose of the limited liability company. It includes details like the nature of business and the product or services rendered. The Statement of Purpose may also include an additional general statement like "and for any other lawful business purpose." This statement helps to cover any changes in the business that may come up later.

Term

Most LLCs have a perpetual lifespan. If there is no specific end date in sight for your business, the operating agreement will indicate that the company will continue to exist unless dissolved according to state laws or the manner described in the operating agreement. For limited liability companies that are formed for a specific purpose and will only exist for a given period or until a specific event occurs, this should be included in the operating agreement as well.

Tax Treatment

The document must indicate how the company elects to be taxed. An LLC may pay tax as a sole proprietorship, as a partnership, or as a corporation.

Percentages of Ownership

In the case of a multi-member LLC, the members are people who have made financial or asset contributions to the business in exchange for a percentage of ownership of the Limited Liability Company. The operating agreement should indicate the percentage of ownership each member gets for their contribution. The default arrangement by state laws is equal membership rights among members. But in the operating agreement, ownership may be divided as the members see fit. Usually, the percentage of ownership will be determined based on the capital contributions of each member.

Admission of New Members

It is common for the membership of an LLC to increase with time. This agreement also outlines the process by which new members will be accepted into the company and how interests will be allocated. If this part of the agreement is not included from the start, you will have to create a new operating agreement that includes it if you finally decide to adopt members.

Other Provisions of the Operating Agreement

In addition to these basic provisions, the operating agreement of a Limited Liability Company may also include additional provisions. Some of these include details of the business or membership of the company itself, such as:

- **Identification of Members and Managers:** The operating agreement is expected to contain the names of all the initial business members along with their titles and addresses. If the LLC is manager-managed, the details of the managers should be included as well.

- **Capital Contributions of Each Member:** The operating agreement is also expected to include the initial capital contributed by each member. The capital may be in the form of cash, assets, or service rendered towards the company formation.

- **Additional Capital Contributions:** This applies more specifically to companies that have raised capital through additional contributions. If the members are not required to make any more contributions, this should be stated in the agreement. However, if an additional contribution is made, the interest percentage for each member's contribution should be included.

- **Distribution of Profits and Losses:** Usually, the distribution of profit and loss is based on the interest percentage of each business member. The specific format for this should be indicated in the agreement. The frequency of profit distribution should also be indicated in the agreement.

- **Member Meetings and Voting Rights:** For a multiple-member Limited Liability Company, you must indicate when and how meetings will take place. Details of the voting rights of members and how votes will be taken should also be worked out among members and included in the agreement. For instance, it is important to state the minimum number of members that must be present to form a quorum and how many votes will be required to approve a decision. Members also have to decide if all the owners will get equal voting rights (I.e., one vote per person) or if the votes will be allocated based on the interest percentage of each member. Other relevant questions include if a unanimous or majority vote will be required to decide and the maximum or the minimum number of votes needed for a quorum, among other things.

- **Management:** One of the fundamental details of an LLC that must be determined beforehand is whether it will be member-managed or managed by a manager. If a manager is to be appointed, the agreement must state the process of electing a manager, the manager's tenure, and how much authority they have over the business. Typically, a manager gets to control daily operational decisions regarding the business, but major decisions are still subject to the approval of a quorum of members. The type of actions that will require the approval of the members will also be stated in the operating agreement.

- **Responsibilities and Compensation of Members:** If members of the company are required to perform any duties in operating the company, the agreement should state whether or not they get additional compensation for their services and how much they get.

- **Admission or Withdrawal of Members:** In later years, there may be a need to admit new members into the business. The operating agreement should indicate details of this process if there will be any. Also, if a member needs to withdraw or be expelled from the company, the document must indicate the procedure for this process.

- **Transfer of Interest:** If a member of the LLC decides to transfer his or her interest, the operating agreement has to provide a "right of first refusal" clause for the other members. This gives the other members the right to buy-out the departing member's interests, based on the terms offered by a third-party buyer.

- **Death of a Member:** Another common provision of the operating agreement is what happens in the event of the death of an

LLC member. There is a need to work out what becomes of the interests of such a member. The members may decide that the interest is automatically transferred to an heir of the dead member or if a first-refusal clause will be available for members to stop the transfer. Some agreements may also allow a transfer while giving the new transferee only rights to the profits but no controlling share on business decisions.

• **Dissolution of the Business:** Finally, the operating agreement is expected to highlight the conditions for the dissolution of the business and how it will be carried out if there is a need for it.

This sums up all the major provisions of the operating agreement of a Limited Liability Company. Although this is not an exhaustive list (since specific details of the agreement may vary from one company to the other), this is a general template that can be used to prepare the agreement. There may still be some additional legal and tax considerations that apply to your LLC agreement. You may wish to speak to a professional to have these additional details hammered out according to your needs.

PART THREE: Operating Your LLC

Chapter Nine: Setting Up Your LLC Accounting

Accounting is one of the essential skills needed by owners or managers of a Limited Liability Company. This is because accurate and comprehensive accounting is needed to preserve the limited liability status of the company. Proper record-keeping is needed to protect the personal assets of Limited Liability Company members from seizure to pay debts or settle legal disputes.

Skills like marketing, sales, and accounting are key administrative components of running a new LLC. By default, limited liability companies are not taxed as corporations, which makes them a popular choice for small business owners. They also require less record keeping compared to a corporation, yet they offer the same level of asset protection.

The bookkeeping requirements for a Limited Liability Company vary from state to state. For instance, some states require LLCs to file an annual report while others do not. But in most cases, keeping a comprehensive account of the daily business transactions is compulsory. Good knowledge of the taxation process is required. You don't want to run into trouble with the IRS. This is why you should seek the advice of a tax professional who can advise you on how an LCC is taxed, at both federal and state levels.

Do I Need a Business Bank Account for my LLC accounting?

Once the process of registering your new Limited Liability Company has been completed, you will need to open a separate bank account for your business. Some banks allow you to open business accounts even before the articles of organization have been approved. No matter the size of your new LLC and the membership structure, you are required by law to open a business account.

In choosing a bank to open your business account, some of the important considerations include the type of account that you need to open and what fees the bank charges to open a small business account. You will also need to know if the bank has branches or ATMs close to your business location or if you can bank online. There are two main types of business accounts you can open for your Limited Liability Company: a business checking account or a business savings account.

• Business Checking Account: a business checking account is used to receive payment from your customers or clients and to pay business expenses.

• Business Savings Account: you use this type of account to save a part of your business your income which will be used to make tax payments or ease the pains of the tax season. Money in your business savings account will come in handy in cases of emergency business expenses.

I also recommend getting a business credit card. Although not a type of bank account in itself, a business credit card can be used to build a good credit score for your business. You only need to ensure that you are paying up your balance in full at the end of every month. You can also earn cash-back and points for your business if you choose the right card, and you perform well on repayment.

Should I Keep My Personal and Business Finances Separate?

As the owner or member of limited liability, you *must* keep your personal finances completely separate from your business finances.

This is one of the primary reasons why a separate business account is needed for your LLC. Keeping personal finance separate from your business finance means you do not pay for any business expenses from your personal account or pay for personal expenses from the business account. Also, avoid transferring cash from your business accounts to your personal account for any reason.

Keeping your accounts separate this way will simplify your accounting process and make it a lot easier to do your taxes. Doing this will ensure that all your business expenses are in one place, and you don't have to sift through personal banking statements to track down your business expenses. It saves you a lot of stress and helps to keep things simple.

The General Ledger

The general ledge is the basic accounting tool for a Limited Liability Company and most of the other business types. A general ledger is similar to a checkbook in that it shows the day-to-day transactions of the company. Besides showing cash received or paid by the business, items like investment assets, valuable equipment, and real estate belonging to the business are also recorded in the general ledger. This document also details the loans, credit, and other liabilities of the business.

Keeping a comprehensive general ledger forms the core of business accounting for a Limited Liability Company. This document provides a detailed picture of all the financial transactions of the business. The information contained in your general ledger can also serve regulatory purposes, especially if you operate in a heavily regulated industry. Since the general ledger contains data for a comprehensive audit of your business activities, it will be a valuable document to show potential investors or buyers if you need to sell your business at some point in the future.

Choosing Tax Treatment

One of the most crucial aspects of setting up a comprehensive accounting system for your business is choosing the way your Limited Liability Company will pay tax. The decision on how the LLC will be taxed has to be made at the point of forming the company. A Limited Liability Company can elect to pay tax as a corporation or choose to pay pass-through tax like a sole proprietorship or partnership business. Even if you are using accounting software to handle your business accounting, you will be asked to indicate how your business entity will be taxed.

If the LLC members elect that the company will be taxed as a pass-through entity, they are required to pay employment taxes from their income at both federal and state levels. At the end of the business year, the owner of such an LLC must include a Schedule C form along with their federal income tax, or a Form 1065 in the case of a multi-member LLC that opts to pay tax as a partnership. For limited liability companies that elect to pay taxes as corporations, they need to fill the Form 1120.

Chapter Ten: Steps for Setting Up Accounting for an LLC

Once you have put in place all the fundamental considerations discussed so far, setting up accounts for your Limited Liability Company is straightforward and easy. First, you need to create a chart of your accounts. This is expected to include all the revenue that comes into the business and the expenses. You should also include the assets and liabilities of the business as well as the owner's equity accounts.

All transactions relating to the business must be recorded. This includes income received, equity withdrawn, written checks, and equity added; each of these is known as a "journal entry." If your journal entries are comprehensive and complete, you should be able to balance your accounts using the equation below.

Assets (A) = Liabilities (L) + Equity (E).

Accounting Methods

There are two fundamental accounting methods for a Limited Liability Company. You can choose to use the cash accounting method or the accrual method. Each of these has specific advantages and disadvantages.

The Cash Method

In this method, the record depends on whether cash has been received or paid out. You do not deduct expenses in your books until you have actually made a payment, and you do not add cash until payment has been received.

The Accrual Method

In this method, expenses and income are recorded the moment a sale occurs even if cash is yet to be received or paid out by the business. For instance, if you complete a project in January and send the client the invoice, but you don't get paid until June, you will record the payment in January when the invoice is sent. However, if you use the cash method, then the payment will only be recorded when you receive the payment in June.

The cash method of accounting is more favored by small business owners, largely due to its simplicity. The accrual method is slightly more complex. However, it paints a more accurate picture of the monthly revenue and expenses of a business.

Another advantage of the cash method is that it helps to delay taxes until you have the funds in hands. With the accrual method, you need to pay taxes of every transaction in the book even if you are yet to receive payment, but with the cash method, you will be taxed only on money that your business has received. Members of the LLC must decide on which accounting system will offer more benefit to the business, and this will be included in the company operating agreement. This lets the accounting staff know which method to use for tax preparation purposes.

The Accounting Cycle

Accounting for a Limited Liability Company follows the same accounting cycle as any other business. Transactions are recorded in journal entries as soon as they occur. Every entry is recorded according to the accounting method in use. Adjusting entries may also be made after the fact. These adjusting entries help to keep the accounts updated to ensure accuracy at the end of the accounting period. The accounting records are closed for the year after the adjusting entries have been made.

Just before closing the accounting books for the year, the accountant prepares the company financial statements, including the income statement, balance sheet, and statement of equity, based on the financial records. These first two records are the same for all types of limited liability, whether multi-member or owned by a single individual. The owner's equity statement must include each company member's investment in the case of a multiple-member LLC. This balance is then adjusted based on the income and loss and withdrawals of each member. We will discuss the process of creating financial statements in greater detail in the next chapter.

Choosing an Accounting System for your Business

There are several ways to organize accounting for your company. Although some people still make use of regular paper bookkeeping ledgers available for sale at office supply stores, more modern options are now available. There are electronic systems to organize accounting for your business. The most basic example includes simple spreadsheet programs like Excel. You can also opt for bookkeeping software like Expensify or QuickBooks, which come with specific features tailored towards making accounting easy for businesses.

Software designed for bookkeeping includes features that allow you to easily prepare income and expenditure reports for your business when you need to. Some of them also allow you to synchronize data from your bank accounts or merchant services that you use to receive payment, for more comprehensive accounting. This simplifies the entire accounting process. It also makes it easier to do your taxes since you simply transfer all the information to your tax adviser to get your year-end report and tax returns ready.

I wouldn't want to pitch any accounting software system as being the best. No matter what your choice, just choose a system that is regularly maintained. You also need a system that is simple to understand with no technical challenges. A system with lots of features is great, but you should take simplicity and effectiveness over systems with too many features that you rarely need.

Setting Up your Accounting System

Most standard accounting software has internal spreadsheets already included in the system. You will be prompted to complete the bank and vendor information as required. Even if you are using a manual paper spreadsheet, you should include a file tab that includes this account information. This way, you will not need other documents while working on your bookkeeping.

Bookkeeping software usually uses one ledger to keep payables and receivables. If you are working manually, you can decide to set up your records this way or not. While some people prefer to see all the running totals of their business, if you find extra columns of data overwhelming, then you should keep separate ledgers for payments and receipts. You should also include a column for client or supplier name, account number, date invoice was sent, payment date, and the expense category. This will make it easier to track transactions.

Also, if you are using one spreadsheet to track both the income and expenditures, you can enter income in one column and expenses in another. Then, the spreadsheet can be set up to deduct the expenses from the running balance of your system.

Other Bookkeeping Items

Besides tracking the income and expenses, which are the fundamental accounting details you need to track, there are other bookkeeping aspects you need to track as well. Some other bookkeeping items you should be familiar with include sales tracking systems, payroll expenses, and inventory.

A sales tracking spreadsheet helps to track information like the amount or quantity of items sold, their retail prices, and how much of the product was sold. It may also include the name of the person that made the sale. An inventory tracking spreadsheet makes it possible to track the number of products available in stock. Some electronic spreadsheets have all these features and can track and sync data across all these spreadsheets. For instance, when an item is recorded as sold in a sales spreadsheet, it is automatically deducted from the inventory. However, on some accounting software, you have to manually copy data across all the spreadsheets.

Setting up Payroll

Another essential part of bookkeeping for companies is setting up payroll. As a one-man Limited Liability Company, this might not be necessary. But as your business grows, you may need to hire contractors, freelancers, or even in-house staff to ease the workload. At this stage, your payroll will become a small but vital part of your accounting efforts. To do this, you will most likely need a payroll spreadsheet.

The essential part of this process is classifying your workers correctly. This is mostly for tax reasons. You may run into trouble with the IRS if you do not fill in your employee payroll correctly.

There are two main categories of workers. An employee is a worker hired by your business over whom you have financial and behavioral control. The company sets the working hours, work conditions, and duties of an employee. A contractor, on the other hand, is an independent worker. Payment for contractors is usually arranged on an hourly or project basis. Once you have your workers classified in this way, you need to be familiar with employment tax laws and put this into consideration in preparing your payroll.

How to Handle Accounting for your Business

As you can see, handling accounting for a Limited Liability Company can be a Herculean task. It involves tracking the business's day-to-day transactions, managing sales and purchases, assets, and liabilities. To do all of these well, you need to develop a working system to handle your accounting. There are three main options for this: you can choose to handle your accounting yourself, outsource the process to a third party, or hire an in-house accountant.

1. DIY Accounting: As a small LLC business just starting, doing accounting yourself is most likely the best option for you. As a one-man Limited Liability Company, you are probably going to be running all the aspects of the business yourself anyway. So, you might as well add accounting to the mix. You probably won't be earning enough to hire someone else anyway, and the volume of accounting should be small enough for you to handle yourself. A multi-member LLC may also have one member handling accounting as part of their responsibilities to the business.

2. Outsourcing: If no member of the LLC is good with numbers, or you simply have too much on your plate already, you can decide to outsource accounting. This can be in the form of hiring a freelancer or part-time bookkeeper. There are also several agencies offering online accounting and bookkeeping services.

3. Hire an In-House Accountant: As your business continues to grow and the workload becomes more difficult to handle on your own, you may hire an accountant in-house. This is the priciest option, but the most convenient of all if you can afford it.

Should I Hire a Small Business Accountant?

If you don't have enough time on your hand to handle your business finances, you may decide to hire an accountant to manage the process for you. In many cases, you may not need the accountant to oversee all aspects of your company finances, just the bookkeeping and report preparation. But even if you are not hiring an in-house accountant, it's a good idea to consult with an accountant for the accounting aspect of your business. Even before your business kicks off, an accountant can help you figure out the legal and financial structure of your business, the type of tax billing you should choose, how to file your tax returns, and so on.

Some of the aspects of your business an accountant can help you with include:

- Developing your financial strategy
- Preparation of financial reports
- Oversight of over-taxation planning and filing
- Ensuring that your business is tax compliant
- Negotiating business transactions and deals.

Wrapping Up

Good accounting habits and practices are vital to the success of your business. Keeping your records correctly and comprehensively will protect you from liabilities. You will also be a lot happier if you don't have to pay your tax preparer loads of money to comb through a box full of invoices and receipts in order to prepare your taxes. No matter the type of Limited Liability Company you are forming or the management structure you adopt, having a solid plan for accounting is super important.

Although laws regarding accounting and tax preparation may vary from one state to the other, all states require you to retain the records of all your transactions for at least three years. It is in your best interest that you comply with this and other accounting requirements. And if you don't know enough to handle it yourself, you should hire a professional to handle the process for you.

Chapter Eleven: Creating Your Financial Statements

Has your business succeeded or failed for the year? The annual financial statements are designed to answer that question. They provide a picture of your company's financial position for a fiscal year. Creating financial statements is one of the most important activities involved in managing a Limited Liability Company. Aside from its usefulness for planning the future of your business, financial statements are also important for tax purposes. In this chapter, I will explain various accounting terms associated with creating financial statements and go over the process of creating one.

What are the financial statements?

The financial statements of a company contain information about the operational results, financial position, and the organization's cash flow. The information contained in the financial statements is used to estimate the company's liquidity, funding, and debt position.

Annual financial statements are prepared for the public (in case of a publicly-traded company) but more specifically for taxation authorities who use the financial statement for the company's tax assessment. The statements are regulated by the IRS and the U.S. Securities and Exchange Commission. It summarizes the company's profits and losses and may also be used to calculate the company's income tax.

As a manager or owner of a Limited Liability Company, you are expected to file annual financial statements as part of your annual report for the company. For public companies, annual reports are available for any member of the public who requests it. For limited liability companies, you are required to file an annual report with the Secretary of State in your company's home state. This document is also made available for company shareholders, who can use the information in the statement to assess the security of their investments. Potential investors may also check financial statements before buying into the company.

Financial statements are also useful for internal communication. Since it provides an overview of the company's financial situation, it ensures transparency and accountability as it clearly shows how the company's capital was used. It can be used to measure the success or failure of a company's management. However, the results of the financial statement aren't the only thing that counts. A bad financial appraisal for the year does not always mean that the managers have done a terrible job. An in-depth look at the figures will reveal where the issues are and help in formulating a plan to plug these areas.

Who needs to prepare annual financial statements?

Publicly traded companies must prepare financial statements and make the details available to the public. Limited liability companies and corporations must also prepare financial statements and file them with the Secretary of State's office in the state where the company operates. Regulations for submitting financial statements and deadlines may vary from state to state. You must be familiar with the rules regarding financial statements in the state where your company operates. For sole proprietorships and simple partnerships, financial statements are not needed. A single income statement is usually all that you need to submit to tax authorities.

What makes up financial statements?

The financial statements of a company are expected to be a precise and comprehensive statement of a company's finances. For a Limited Liability Company, the two most important components of financial statements are the income statements and the balance sheet. Other documents that you need to include in the financial statements include a cash flow statement and a statement of changes in stockholder equity.

By comparing financial statements from various fiscal periods, it is possible to track the growth of a company. Although working on financial statements usually involves sitting down and assembling the related data into a specific format, in a real sense, the process of creating your financial statements begins with day to day bookkeeping. If you have been keeping comprehensive and accurate daily records, creating your financial statements will be as simple as pulling together all the information you already have. You will have trouble creating your financial statements if your books are incomplete. In this case, the process of creating your financial statements will have to begin by updating your books.

Now that you are familiar with what financial statements are, let's talk about the specific process of creating the various components of a financial statement.

Creating a Balance Sheet

The balance sheet is a summary of a company's financial situation for a given period. It lists everything a company owns, and everything it owes then calculates the difference between the figures to show the company's net worth.

To create a balance sheet for your Limited Liability Company, you need to list all your assets on the left side of the page. This includes everything your company owns, from the cash you have at hand to anything in your bank accounts. Your assets also include all your accounts receivable (what your customers owe you.) The values of equipment owned by the company and other assets must be estimated as well and added to the financial worth of the business.

One the right side of the balance sheet, the liabilities of the business are listed. This includes all the amounts the company is owing, including both short term and long-term debts. Credit card balances and bank loans should also be included in this part of the balance sheet. Accounts payable, unpaid supplies, and shipments already received are also part of the business liabilities.

The assets and liabilities are totaled separately. Then the liabilities are subtracted from the assets of the business. Whatever is left after subtracting the liabilities from the assets is the owner's equity. This is then added to the right side of the balance sheet. Once the owner's equity has been added to the liability column, you should be able to balance the balance sheet. This means the assets will be equal to your liabilities (at least on paper).

Steps for Preparing your Income Statement

To prepare the income statement for a Limited Liability Company, you must understand the individual components and know how to tie them all together.

1. Sales: This is a figure that represents how much revenue the business has generated for the period under consideration. The amount to be recorded in this section is the total figure for sales made minus sales discounts and any products returned.

2. Cost of Goods Sold: The cost of goods sold represents the direct costs of producing or acquiring the products you sell. This includes the cost of materials that were purchased from suppliers to be used for manufacturing the product. The internal expenses of your manufacturing process are added here.

3. For service businesses where no products are manufactured or purchased, the cost of goods sold will only include your expenses incurred in the process of supplying the service. If you own the company and you do not take additional salary beyond the company's

profits, then the service expenses will be zero. But, if you receive a salary from the business or you need to hire someone to offer the service, then labor costs will be added to the cost of goods sold section.

4. Gross Profit: To calculate the gross profit, you need to subtract the cost of goods sold from the sales. The income taxes and the operating expenses of the business are not included here.

5. Operating Expenses: Operating expenses are daily expenses that are incurred in the day-to-day operation of the business. They are in two broad categories: marketing costs and general or administrative expenses. Some of the possible operating expenses include:

- **Sales Salaries:** This includes the salaries, bonuses, or commissions paid to sales staff during the period under review

- **Collateral and Promotion:** These are expenses incurred by the business for the purchase or creation of sales materials used by the sales staff for business marketing. Promotions fees also include product samples or giveaways used for promotional purposes.

- **Advertising:** This includes the cost of multimedia advertisements for the company. This can be in terms of the cost of creating advertisement materials and the cost of placing the adverts.

- **Other Sales Costs:** You may include other costs associated with selling your products not covered in other sections here. This may include travel costs, client meals, cost of organizing sales meetings, and other miscellaneous costs.

Administrative Expenses

◆ **Office Salaries:** Salaries for part-time and full-time office workers

◆ **Rent:** Fee incurred on renting or leasing office, industrial, or warehouse space

◆ **Utilities:** This includes the cost of utilities like heating, electricity, internet services, phone usage, and so on.

◆ **Depreciation:** Depreciation refers to the loss in value of equipment owned by the company and used by the business. Assets and equipment belonging to a company that may become depreciated over time include computers, office buildings, furniture, and so on.

◆ **Other Overhead Costs:** Any other operating expenses that cannot fit into any of the other categories may be included here. Examples of such expenses are the cost of cleaning services, office supplies, insurance, and so on.

6. **Total Expenses:** Covers the total of all the expenses spent on running the business excluding interest or tax expenses

7. **Net Income before Taxes:** It represents how much the business has earned as income before income taxes are paid. You arrive at this figure by subtracting the total expenses from the company's gross profit.

8. **Taxes:** The income taxes owed by the business at Federal, state, or local levels are included here.

9. **Net Income:** The net income is how much the company has left after the income taxes have been paid.

Statement of Retained Earnings

The statement of retained earnings is also known as the statement of changes in equity. This statement forms an integral part of financial statements for corporations and limited liability companies. Although a statement of changes in equity is not required to prepare consolidated financial statements, its purpose is to show changes in equity between two fiscal periods.

The statement of retained earnings is expected to reflect all changes (whether upward or downward) in the company equity. The statement of equity changes provides context for the balance sheet using the content of the income statement. This statement is a requirement under the United States Generally Accepted Accounting Principles (US GAAP) in cases when the income statements and the comparative balance sheets are provided together.

Although there are no strict rules under commercial law on how this document should be structured, the statement of equity changes is expected to include the issued capital, capital reserve, retained earnings, annual profits, and the revaluation reserves. The information included in this statement is compiled from values from the previous year. It shows the key dates and events that led to the changes. At the end of the statement, the figures from the last key date and new figures should be displayed in the report. The result is a clear and concise table that shows all the changes in equity.

Cash Flow Statement

The cash flow statement should be included in any financial statement. Even if this statement is not compulsory, it is an important document, and it is recommended that you prepare it. The aim of preparing the cash flow statement is to indicate the cash flow between two reporting periods.

A cash flow statement shows the movement of all funds affecting a company's liquidity. This statement provides additional information about the flow of cash within a company, more than the income statement or balance sheet do.

Accounting is done through two major methods, i.e., through the accrual method or the cash accounting method. Most limited liability companies make use of the accrual method. In this case, the income statement in the yearly financial report does not represent the true cash position of the company. It is the cash flow statement that can truly reveal this since it focuses more on cash accounting.

Even though your business is profitable based on the income statement, you may still be failing in terms of cash flow management. For instance, a company that sells products on credit to its customers will record the sale as revenue even though cash has not been received. Consequently, you will need to pay income taxes on the profit on the items sold on credit based on the figures in the income statement. This is why the cash flow statement is important. It is a critical tool for analysts and investors in a business.

The cash flow statement has three components. They are:

Cash Flow from Operating Activities (CFO)

This is the first section of the cash flow statement. The cash flow from operations reports the flow of cash directly from the main business activities. This includes cash flow and outflows from activities like sales and purchases, employee payment, utilities, and so on. This section begins with the net income but then reconciles all the non-cash items relating to operational activities to the cash items. The cash flow from operations is essentially a statement of net income but in cash form. Generally, it is expected that a company can generate enough positive cash flow from its operational activities. If the cash flow generated is not sufficient enough, the company may need to seek financing from external sources for growth and expansion to be possible.

Cash Flow from Investment Activities (CFI)

The second section of a cash flow statement considers cash flows from the company's investments. It reports the cash flow as a result of gains or losses on investments. In this section, cash spent on property or equipment owned by the company is recorded. The main purpose of cash flow from the investing section is to track changes in capital expenditures. An increase in capital expenditure indicates a reduction in cash flow for this section. However, this isn't always a bad thing. An increase in capital expenditure could mean the company is making more investments into its future operations. High capital expenditure is usually an indicator of growth.

Although positive cash flow from investing can be good, many investors prefer companies that can generate adequate cash flow from their business operations directly.

Cash Flow from Financing Activities (CFF)

This is the final section of a cash flow statement. This section provides an overview of cash that is being used to finance the business. Typically, it measures cash flow between a company and its owners and creditors. The source of cash flow in this section is typically from equity or debt, while outflow can be because of loan repayment or dividends.

The cash flow from financing section is used by analysts to determine how much a company paid out through share buybacks or dividends. It can also be used to determine how the company raised cash to drive its operational growth.

Positive CFF indicates that more money is coming into the business than going out. Similarly, a negative figure could mean that the business is paying more debt or making dividend payments to shareholders.

Cash flow can be calculated through either direct or indirect methods.

The Direct Method

The direct method of preparing income statements involves calculating cash outflows and inflows directly from the cash flow of various business transactions. In this method, the cash flow is recorded directly based on the outgoing and incoming payments. The balance of these payments results in your cash flow statement. The items are marked according to their respective purposes.

The Indirect Method

This method involves deriving the information for cash flow statements from the annual financial statement. To do this, the income statement for all the non-cash transactions will have to be adjusted. The indirect method is only used for cash from the operating activities section. Cash flow from investing and financing is determined with the direct method.

Prepare Closing Entries to Get the Books Ready for the Next Accounting Period

After preparing your financial statement at the end of the fiscal year, there are still some simple tasks you need to complete. You need to prepare your accounts for the next accounting year. This involves preparing your closing entries by clearing out the expenses and income accounts in the general ledger then transferring the net income to the equity account.

Note that closing entries are quite different from adjusting entries. You need to adjust entries to update certain accounts in the general ledger at the end of a fiscal period. This is usually done before you begin to prepare your financial statement and your income tax return. Closing endings, on the other hand, is done to clear out income and expenses account at the start of a new accounting year.

Preparing your closing entries is a very straightforward process. Here are some tips to follow:

1. Close the Revenue Accounts: To do this, simply prepare a journal entry that debits all the revenue accounts. These accounts should have a credit balance in your general ledger before the closing entry. Prepare an account and call it "income summary," then credit it.

2. Close the Expense Account: Prepare another journal entry that credits the expense accounts. These accounts should be on a debit balance in your general ledger before you close the entry. Debit the income summary account for this total.

3. Transfer the Income Summary Balance to a Capital Account: For this, you will need to prepare a journal entry to clear out the income summary account. This entry will transfer the net income or loss of the business to the equity account.

4. Close the Drawing Account: If there is a drawing account, close it by preparing a journal entry that credits the accounts and debits the equity account.

Chapter Twelve: How to File Your Taxes as an LLC

As for filing taxes, a Limited Liability Company acts like a hermit crab. An LLC has no tax classification of its own. Like a hermit crab, it inhabits the tax home of other types of businesses. Limited liability companies can elect to be taxed like one-man businesses, partnerships, or corporations.

Although this tax flexibility is one thing that makes limited liability companies so appealing to business owners, the ever-changing nature of taxes for LLCs can be confusing for someone just starting. You must understand the differences between the various ways LLCs are taxed because the method of taxation can affect your total tax billing and your self-employment tax obligations.

How Are LLCs Taxed?

There is no specific tax classification for limited liability companies. The IRS has not established a unique classification for such companies. This means there is no dedicated LLC tax return form even though LLCs definitely have to pay taxes. To pay taxes, a Limited Liability Company can be treated as an entirely different entity. By default, a single-member LLC will be treated by the IRS like a sole-proprietorship while a multiple-member LLC is treated as a general partnership. However, every LLC can choose the preferred way they want to be taxed by filling a form with the IRS, which changes their tax status. The LLC may elect how it will be taxed at the time of its formation or make the election for tax classification at a later date.

Filing Tax Returns as a Single-Member LLC

For a single-member Limited Liability Company, the IRS treats your company as a sole proprietorship. In this case, the company itself is not taxed. Rather the owner of the LLC pays tax on his or her business profits like a sole proprietor does. You are expected to report your income and expenses on a Schedule C form, which is a personal tax return form. As the owner, you will also list the profit and loss of the business on the income section of your Form 1040, which is the U.S. Individual Income Tax Return form.

An LLC treated like a sole proprietorship is ignored for tax purposes. Such a company is also known as a "disregarded entity." The LLC still retains its limited liability status and only enjoys a " disregarded entity" status for tax purposes.

Multi-Member LLCs Taxed Like Partnerships

The IRS automatically treats a Limited Liability Company with more than one member as a partnership for tax purposes. In this case, the Limited Liability Company income will flow through to its members and will be reported on their personal tax returns.

But the company itself is not taxed. LLCs taxed as a partnership are expected to file Form 1065. This is an informational tax return form that reports the income and expenses of a partnership. The individual members of the Limited Liability Company are also issued a Schedule K-1 form. This indicates each member's share of the total profit of the LLC, per the company's operating agreement.

The LLC members also fill out a Schedule E form with their personal tax returns, reporting their share of the business profit or loss. Members are expected to report and pay taxes on their share of the business profits even if they decide to leave a percentage in the business as a form of reinvestment.

Self-Employment Taxes and Estimated Taxes

In the eyes of the IRS, members of limited liability companies taxed as partnerships or sole proprietorships are considered self-employed. For someone that works for an employer, the employer is expected to pay half of their Medicare and social security taxes while the employee pays the other half. But for self-employed individuals, the full amount must be paid by the individual since you are your own employer. However, while filing the annual tax return, a self-employed person is allowed to deduct half of the tax from their income. This helps to offset the impact of the self-employment tax in the long run.

You are expected to file a Schedule SE form with your tax return. This is a self-employment tax form that is used to report and calculate self-employment tax. You are also expected to make an estimated payment of these taxes along with your personal income taxes every quarter. You may be fined or penalized if you fail to do this when due.

LLC Taxed as S Corp. or C Corp

Besides the default system of taxation used for LLCs, a Limited Liability Company may also elect to be taxed as a corporation. Corporate taxation is not as straightforward as being taxed as a partnership or sole proprietorship. It is a good idea to consult with an accounting expert before choosing this system of taxation. LLCs that opt to be taxed as corporations may do so because:

- They intend to leave a substantial amount in the business every year as a way of financing future expansion plans.
- They want to minimize self-employment taxes because the company makes more profits than the amount the business owners should make in a salary.

To put this into effect, you are expected to file Form 8832 with the IRS; this is an Entity Classification Election form. When this is done, the IRS automatically treats the LLC as a C-corporation. However, you can take things a bit further by electing to be taxed as an S corporation.

An LLC that elects to be taxed as a C corporation is expected to file a corporate tax return every year. The members of the company are also expected to report all their earnings in terms of salaries and dividends on their personal tax returns.

An LLC taxed as an S corporation follows a flow-through tax system. This system is similar to how partnerships pay tax. In this case, you are expected to file an information return and provide the company's members with a Schedule K-1 form which indicates their share of the business profits or loss. Each member is expected to report their income on Schedule E of the personal tax returns.

For small businesses that are just starting out, being taxed as a sole-proprietorship or partnership is the most recommended option. However, as your business grows, you may need to consult with an accounting expert to figure out the potential benefits of switching to corporate taxation for your LLC. In either case, you must know when and how to file an estimated annual tax form for your limited liability company to avoid being penalized or fined.

Should I File a Tax Return for an LLC With No Activity?

Sometimes, it is possible that your Limited Liability Company does not record any business activity for a business year. For instance, a newly formed LLC yet to start doing business or an older one that has become inactive but without formal dissolution. However, even if your Limited Liability Company is inactive for a year, which means there is no income or expenses for that year, you might still need to file a Federal income tax return. The requirements for filing tax returns for an inactive LLC depends largely on the system of taxation the LLC used. That is, whether you are being taxed as a corporation or treated as a disregarded entity.

Filing Requirements for Inactive Disregarded Entities

LLCs treated as partnerships or sole proprietorship are known as disregarded entities by the IRS. In this case, the income and expenses are reported as self-employment income by the members, and the taxes are paid accordingly. For a single-member company that reports no business activity for the year, there are no expenses to deduct. Hence, the members need not file a Schedule C to report the company income. However, the members will still need to file a personal tax return if he or she had another source of income within the period under review. In this case, a Schedule C will be filed for self-employment income from other businesses.

Filing Requirements for an inactive LLC Partnership

An LLC that is taxed as a partnership is treated the same way as other partnerships as far as federal income tax is concerned. Such a Limited Liability Company is expected to file an information partnership tax return unless it receives no income within a business year, and no expenses were recorded. In this case, there can be no claims of credits or deductions. So, unless there are expenses or credits the LLC wants to claim, it does not need to file a tax return.

LLC Tax Filing Requirements for an Inactive LLC Taxed as a Corporation

The rules for filing taxes for an inactive LLC being taxed as a corporation are slightly different from that of partnerships or sole proprietorships in the same situation. In the case of a corporation, you are expected to file a corporate tax return even if you have no income for the year. Hence, for LLCs that have elected to be taxed as corporations, you are expected to file a Federal income tax return even if the business was inactive throughout the year.

Even if your business is inactive during a business year, you are expected to understand how tax filing works for your company, so as to avoid fines and penalties.

Handling Tax-Deductibles for Limited Liability Companies

If you intend to start a Limited Liability Company, there are several expenses that you will have to cover on your own as part of the process of setting up your company. The good news, however, is that the IRS offers an opportunity for startups to claim tax deductions on business-startup expenses when they file their taxes each year.

According to the Federal tax code, owners of limited liability companies are allowed to deduct startup expenses and operational expenses that the business incurs before it becomes fully operational. This is applicable no matter the type of tax structure that the LLC adopts. But what exactly are these startup costs that businesses are allowed to claim deductibles on?

What Are Startup Costs?

Startup costs are expenses incurred by a startup in the early stages of its development. This includes costs like the money spent on creating the company, carrying out a market survey for your new business, marketing or promoting your new business, travel expenses, fees for training new employees, and so on. It essentially includes all the costs incurred before your first transaction with a client or customer.

The largest form of startup cost is organizational expenses. These are expenses involved in the registration process of a Limited Liability Company. They include attorneys' fees for drafting membership agreement and other costs relating to paperwork for the business. However, not all organizational expenses are tax-deductible; for example, costs of soliciting investors or attorney fees paid for drafting customer contracts, among others.

How Much Can You Deduct?

LLC members are allowed tax deductions on their startup and organizational expenses in the first year of the company's operation. The upper limit of deduction is $5000 of the LLC startup expenses. LLC members are allowed to make this deduction up to the amount of the total cost that is $50,000. Any cost that is over this amount is considered amortizable.

The startup cost deductions must be claimed on the LLC tax return in the same year the expenses were paid. For example, startup expenses for forming your company in 2019 must be deducted when you file your taxes with the IRS in 2020.

How to Amortize Startup Costs

Amortization is the process of spreading costs over multiple pay periods. Startup costs and organizational costs are classified as capital expenditures. Hence, they are subject to amortization rules. You can claim these deductions over 180 months beginning from the date the LLC becomes active. To amortize startup expenses, you need a 4562 Form, describing the company activities, which should be attached to your LLC tax return. You also need to attach a statement to the 4862 form which outlines the specific startup cost you want to amortize. You are expected to include the official date of the formation of your business along with your amortization request.

Conclusion

For filing taxes for limited liability companies, the process is a lot different from paying personal taxes. To avoid issues, you should consult with an accountant or LLC tax specialist to help figure out the best taxation system that will get you the most benefits, and also to find ways to save you money while keeping your business out of trouble with the tax authorities.

Chapter Thirteen: Setting Up Payroll and Paying Yourself

Congratulations! Now you have your Limited Liability Company fully set up and operational. Now, all you have to bother about is the day-to-day running of your business, which I must admit will be a handful. There are still a lot of things you have to do to keep your LLC running. One of those tasks is preparing payroll and paying your staff. In many cases, this also includes paying yourself as the owner of the Limited Liability Company.

Like everything else that involves your LLC, there is a process for this. Payroll for a limited liability company is not exactly the same as that of other business structures. The rules for paying yourself as the owner of an LLC are also different.

Owners of a Limited Liability Company are paid more like independent contractors working for the company than like regular employees of the business. If all the workers in an LLC are members (owners) of the company with no non-member working for the company, as far as the IRS is concerned, the company has no employees. In such a case, you need not prepare payroll or handle any payroll tax obligations. You only have to take on these responsibilities once you hire your first employee. The process of carrying out these tasks depends on the type of employees the company has.

Types of Employees in a Limited Liability Company

There are two broad categories of workers you can have in a Limited Liability Company. They can be non-member employees or member employees.

1. Member Employee: The members of the company are the owners of the Limited Liability Company. Members become part of the company mainly because of their financial investment, in terms of cash or assets. They hold membership interests in the company

2. Non-Member Employees: Non-member employees are people that are hired to work for the company, whether on a part-time or full-time basis. This group of employees is the ones commonly paid through payroll. A special group of non-member employees is contractors or freelancers hired to perform specific tasks for the company. Such contractors are not included in the payroll since they do not receive a regular payment from the company. Instead, contracts are paid via accounts payable.

Payroll Responsibilities of the Employer

An LLC that has employees on its payroll has some simple responsibilities to carry out regarding its employee payroll. These obligations are the same as those of other forms of business. They include:

• **Withholding Federal, State, and Local Taxes on Behalf of the Employee:** It is the responsibility of a limited liability company to withhold some percentage of the employee's wages as tax, which will then be paid to the government directly. The taxes withheld this way are deposited in bank accounts based on the IRS regulations.

- **Filing a Tax Return Quarterly:** The employers are expected to file a tax return and pay the withheld taxes to the government.
- **Sending a Form W2 to Employees:** As an employer, you are also expected to send the form W2 to your employees. This form summarizes the annual earnings of the employee and the taxes withheld.

Mandatory Employer Contribution

Under Federal laws, for every Limited Liability Company with employees, there are three mandatory benefits to which the business must contribute. These are the social security compensations, Medicare, and unemployment contribution.

- **Social Security Benefits:** Every company is expected to pay an additional 6.2% of the employee's salary for social security.
- **Medicare Benefits:** An employer is expected to pay up to 1.5% of an Employee's pay as a Medicare benefit contribution, plus an extra 0.9% for highly compensated individuals.
- **Unemployment Compensation:** Employers are expected to take full responsibility for the unemployment taxes of their employees. The employees make no contributions of their own to this payment. Only the business pays to the Federal Unemployment Tax Act through Federal Payroll Tax Contributions.

The LLC is expected to deposit these employer payroll taxes in the bank, along with the taxes withheld from each employee. The records for this are to be included in the quarterly tax return for the company.

Paying Yourself as the Owner of an LLC

Owners of an LLC business still have to earn a living. This is one of the main reasons you started your business. This means you have to know how to pay yourself from your LLC. There is a protocol for this, and you need to be familiar with it. There are two main ways you can pay yourself as the owner or member of an LLC. You can choose to be treated as an employee and receive wages from the business.

You can also be treated as a member of an LLC. In this case, you receive distributions from the company profits. The process of filing taxes for either case varies.

Members Earning Wages as an LLC Employee

Owners of a Limited Liability Company are not considered employees of the company even if they work for the business. However, the company may provide compensation for services to the company in the form of guaranteed payment.

Paying yourself as an employee of your LLC means you earn compensation quite similar to a salary from the company regularly. This method of payment can be quite beneficial if you seek regular business income throughout the year. However, earning wages this way is not automatic; you must be offering your services to the business in one active capacity or the other. Members with no active responsibilities in the business cannot get paid through this method.

For multiple-member limited liability companies, if one member decides to take payment as an employee, all the members that participate in company operations must be paid this way too. However, if only one member has an active role in the business, then only that member will be paid through this method while the others will only get paid through distributions.

How Taxes are Paid for LLCs That Pay Members as Employees

All employee wages are recorded as part of the Limited Liability Company operating expenses and will be deducted from the company's total profits. However, you should be aware that the tax authorities will only permit reasonable wage deductions. Hence, the salary that members receive for their services to the company must be within the industry norms. In addition to the salaries, members that are also employees can also receive special bonuses for their services.

The W-4 form is filed with the IRS in order to determine how much will be withheld from your pay as payroll withholding tax. The company will pay your salary as a worker and will withhold the expected amount for your employment and income taxes from your salary.

Members that Receive Distributions from the LLC Profits

The second method of getting paid as an LLC member is to collect distributions from the yearly profits made by the LLC. Each member of the Limited Liability Company has a capital account based on their investment in the business. At the end of each business year, the company distributes the profits or losses into each member's account. Members can withdraw from their capital accounts based on the rules of the company's operating agreement.

So, if your Limited Liability Company posts a profit of $200,000 for a business year, and you own 50% of the company's interest, you are liable to receive $100,000 as distribution. For someone who prefers more consistent pay, you could have an arrangement that allows you to be paid ongoing payments against the expected profit at year-end. For example, if the expected profit at the end of the business year is $12,000, you can decide to withdraw $1000 monthly. At the end of the year, the total withdrawals you have made for the year will be removed from the total profit. You will also get any extra left after the deduction has been made. So, if the profit at the end of the year is $20,000, then you will get an additional $8000 at year-end.

How taxes are paid for LLCs that pay members through Distributions from LLC Profits.

For a single-member Limited Liability Company, you will not need to pay income taxes on the distributions you get. You will need to file a Schedule C form with the IRS to report the business profits along with your personal tax returns.

For multiple-member LLCs, the company is treated as a partnership. Each member of the company is expected to report their share of the profit, and they pay the income tax on this profit. A multi-member LLC has to file the IRS form 1065, which is used to report the profit or losses are shared among members.

Members of the LLC already pay tax on the money deposited in their capital account. Hence, distributions are typically not subject to self-employment tax. However, companies may not disguise their guaranteed payment as capital account distribution as a way to avoid the tax burden. Doing this would be illegal.

You should also note that it is possible to receive a monthly salary and also get the end of the year profit distributions. These two are not mutually exclusive. Members of an LLC offering their services to the company are eligible to get paid on both ends.

LLC Members Getting Paid Like Independent Contractors

Another way you, as the owner of a Limited Liability Company, can get paid is by working as an independent contractor for the company. In this case, you are not a regular employee, so you are not captured on the payroll. Instead, you will be paid like an independent contractor that does some work for the company.

For instance, you are the owner of an LLC but you also work independently as a graphics designer. If your company needs to produce some marketing or promotion materials, you may hire your own services as an independent contractor to produce the designs for the company.

But there are not so many benefits to this approach. You will need to file the Form W-9 with the LLC if you choose this method. And the LLC files a Form 1099-MISC at the end of the year. This will require you to pay the self-employment tax on any amount earned in this deal.

Aside from these three options, there is also the option of not receiving payment from the company at all and leaving all your profits in your business. However, in this case, you will still have to pay personal income tax on the total profit earned at the end of the year since the Limited Liability Company profit will be passed through to you on your personal tax return.

Conclusion

If you have made it this far, congratulations; you now know all that there is to know about forming a Limited Liability Company from scratch or converting your existing business to an LLC. Hopefully, you now understand the potential benefits of making such a move, and you can effectively distinguish between what you stand to gain from an LLC compared to other business structures.

The good thing about forming an LLC is the simplicity of the entire process. With this book, I have been able to simplify the process of forming and managing an LLC, along with describing all the tools you need. Of course, there are still some technical aspects of running an LLC that you may find a bit complex. For tasks like accounting, taxes, and even the process of setting up an LLC itself (creating articles of organization and operating agreement), you may have to consult with professionals in this field for further clarification. They will help provide first-hand information about how the process works.

Limited liability companies are probably the most popular form of corporate business structure right now. And for good reasons, too. Now that you have a better understanding of how to form this type of business works, all that's left is to decide to set up an LLC as your chosen business structure. Best of luck on your journey!!!

Glossary of Terms

Accrual Method of Accounting: In this method, expenses and income are recorded the moment a sale occurs even if cash is yet to be received or paid out by the business.

Articles of Organization: The articles of organization of a Limited Liability Company are documents that act as a charter for the existence of a Limited Liability Company in any U.S. state. It is filed with the office of the Secretary of State or any state agency that is in charge of business registration. Basically, this document describes the basic operating characteristics and identifying details of the Limited Liability Company. Filing this document and its consequent approval by the relevant state authority legally creates the LLC and seals its status as a registered company within that state.

Balance Sheet: The balance sheet is a summary of a company's financial situation for a given period. It lists everything a company owns and everything it owes, then calculates the difference between the figures to show the company's net worth.

Business Checking Account: A business checking account is used to receive payment from your customers or clients and to pay business expenses.

Business Savings Account: Using this type of account, a part of your business income can then be used for tax payments or to ease the pain of the tax season. Money in your business savings account will come in handy in cases of emergency business expenses.

Capital Account: The capital account records the individual accounting records of each individual member's investment. This balance is increased based on the initial investment of each member.

Capital Expenditure: This refers to the money a business spends on acquiring and maintaining fixed assets like land, buildings, equipment, and so on.

Cash Flow Statement: A cash flow statement shows the movement of all funds affecting a company's liquidity. This statement provides additional information about the flow of cash within a company more than the income statement and balance sheet do.

Cash Flow from Investing (CFI): The cash flow from investing reports the cash flow as a result of gains or losses on investments. In this section, cash spent on property or equipment owned by the company is recorded. The main purpose of cash flow from the investing section is to track changes in capital expenditures.

Cash Flow from Operations (CFO): The Cash flow from operations reports the flow of cash directly from the main business activities of the company. This includes cash flow and outflows from activities like sales and purchases, employee payment, utilities, and so on.

Cash Method of Accounting: In this method, the record depends on whether cash has been received or paid out. You do not deduct expenses in your books until you have actually made the payment, and you do not add cash until payment has been received.

Corporations: Corporations are businesses that operate as separate legal entities from their owners. Hence, the owners are protected from claims filed against the activities of the company or debts. A corporation is the most complex form of organizational structure for any business. Unlike partnerships and a sole proprietorship, they are taxed as separate entities from the owner by the IRS.

General Ledger: The general ledger is the basic accounting foundation for a Limited Liability Company and most of the other business types. A general ledger is similar to a checkbook in that it shows the day-to-day transactions of the company. In addition to showing cash received or paid by the business, investment assets, valuable equipment, and real estate belonging to the business are also recorded in the general ledger.

Limited Company: In a limited company, the liability borne by company members is limited to their investment in the company. Limited companies are typically of two forms. They can be limited by guarantee or by shares.

Limited Liability Company: A Limited Liability Company falls somewhere in-between all the other types of business structures. It is organized in the form of a sole proprietorship or general partnership but offers a level of legal protection similar to that of limited partnerships or corporations.

Limited Partnerships: A limited partnership is a type of business entity owned by two groups of partners. One group (which can be one person or more) has control over the business, and they are liable for the debt. These are the general partners. The other group of partners only have an investment in the company, but do not participate in the management.

Mandatory Employer Contributions: For every Limited Liability Company with employees, there are three mandatory benefits to which the business must contribute. These are the social security compensations, Medicare, and unemployment contribution.

Manager-Managed Limited Liability Company: In the manager-managed LLC structure, a separate manager will be appointed to manage the day-to-day operations of the business.

Member-Managed Limited Liability Company: A member-managed Limited Liability Company is run directly by the owner(s) of the business.

Multiple Member Limited Liability Company: a multiple-member LLC is a type of LLC that is owned by more than one person.

Non-Statutory Conversion: In this method of business conversion, a new company is formed, and the old company is merged into the newly formed one. Unlike the two other conversion methods, the non-statutory methods of conversion do not automatically transfer assets and liabilities of the corporation to the new LLC. Instead, after forming the LLC, special agreements will have to be formulated to transfer these liabilities and assets. Additionally, special agreements will also be needed for the conversion of corporate shares to membership interests in the new company.

Partnerships: Any business started and run by one or more persons is considered a partnership by the IRS. In the case of a partnership, each person (partner) is considered equally liable. Hence, they share the net profit, loss, and financial obligations of the business.

Registered Agent: A registered agent is someone who sends and receives official paperwork on behalf of a business. He or she receives important legal documents from both state and federal agencies. A registered agent is also in charge of receiving service of process documents for your business. Registered agents are also known as statutory agents or agents of process.

Restricted Limited Liability Company: A restricted liability company is a type of LLC that has some restrictions within the articles of the organization. Notably, the members have to wait ten years before they can receive their distributions from the business.

S Corporation: Subchapter S corporations have less than 100 shareholders. They function more like partnerships because the company's income and loss may be passed on to the shareholders to avoid paying federal taxes.

Series Limited Liability Company: A series LLC provides liability protection for members across multiple series. Each of these series is theoretically free from liabilities that may arise from the activities of other series. Each series comprises business entities that can include members, managers, interests, and assets, each with their designated debts, rights, and obligations.

Single-Member Limited Liability Company: As the names imply, a single-member Limited Liability Company is a type of LLC that is owned by an individual.

Sole Proprietorship: A sole proprietorship has the simplest business organization structure possible. It is a type of business owned and run by one individual. There is no legal distinction between a sole proprietor and the business entity he owns.

Statement of Retained Earnings: The statement of retained earnings is also known as the statement of changes in equity. This statement forms an integral part of financial statements for corporations and limited liability companies. Although a statement of changes in equity is not required to prepare consolidated financial statements, its purpose is to show changes in equity between two fiscal periods.

Statutory Conversion: This method involves filing a document with the secretary of state to change from one business-structure form to the other. With this method, there is no need to form a new entity. The company is converted to a different form entirely, and the assets, liabilities, and ownership interests are automatically transferred. This is the simplest and cheapest way of changing the form of a business entity.

Statutory Merger: This is a method of converting a corporation to a Limited Liability Company that involves an inter-entity merger. Under this approach, a new business entity is formed, and the old entity is then merged into the new one. With the statutory conversion method, the old business entity ceases to exist immediately; the process is completed. The liabilities and assets of the old entity are transferred to the new one.

Subchapter C Corporation: ordinary corporations are regarded as subchapter C corporations. They are considered separate legal entities, and the tax returns are filed separately from shareholders.

Common IRS Forms

Form 8832: This is an Entity Classification Election form. You must complete this form to elect the tax status of your LLC if it is not the assigned default status. You may take this form if you elect to have your company taxed as a C Corporation.

RS Form 2553: This is the "Election by a Small Business Corporation" form. You are required to file this form with the IRS if you wish to switch the status of your LLC from a C corporation to an S corporation for federal taxation purposes.

Form 1040: The IRS form 1040 is a tax form used to file personal income tax. This form is used to calculate a taxpayer's total taxable income and also determines how much the government refunds.

Form 1065: This is the return of partnership income form. All partnerships are expected to file form 1065, whether it is a general partnership, limited partnership, or a Limited Liability Company operating as a partnership.

Form 1120: This is the corporate income tax return form. Corporations use this form to report their income, losses, profits, and credit. Corporations or LLCs being taxed as Corporations use this form to figure out their tax liability.

Disregarded Entity: To report the taxes of your LLC as a disregarded entity, attach a single-member LLC tax form to your 1040:

- Schedule C, Profit or Loss from Business (Sole Proprietorship)

- Schedule C-EZ, Net Profit from Business (Sole Proprietorship)
- Schedule E, Supplemental Income and Loss
- Schedule F, Profit or Loss from Farming

LLCs classified as corporations file one of the following:

- Form 1120, U.S. Corporation Income Tax Return
- Form 1120S, U.S. Income Tax Return for an S Corporation

Schedule K-1 Form: This is an IRS tax form that is issued for investments in partnership. This form reports each partner's share of the profits or losses, either from the partnership business or an LLC taxed as a partnership.

Form W-3: This is the Transmittal of Wage and Tax Statements form. This is not a standalone form. It is filed alongside the Form W-2, and it summarizes the information contained in this form. It provides a compiled list of all the employee information that has been included in the Forms W-2. This form contains details like the amount paid to all employees, the total Federal income, mandatory contributions, and so on.

Form W-2: This is the Wage and Tax Statement. It reports the annual wages of employees in your company. The company is expected to send a copy of this form to its employees. The content of this form includes the wages paid to workers throughout the year. It also shows the gross wages and withheld taxes, among other details.

Form 4562: This is the Depreciation and Amortization tax form of the Internal Revenue Service (IRS). The purpose of this form is to make deductions for the depreciation or amortization of a piece of property.

Here's another book by Robert McCarthy
that you might be interested in

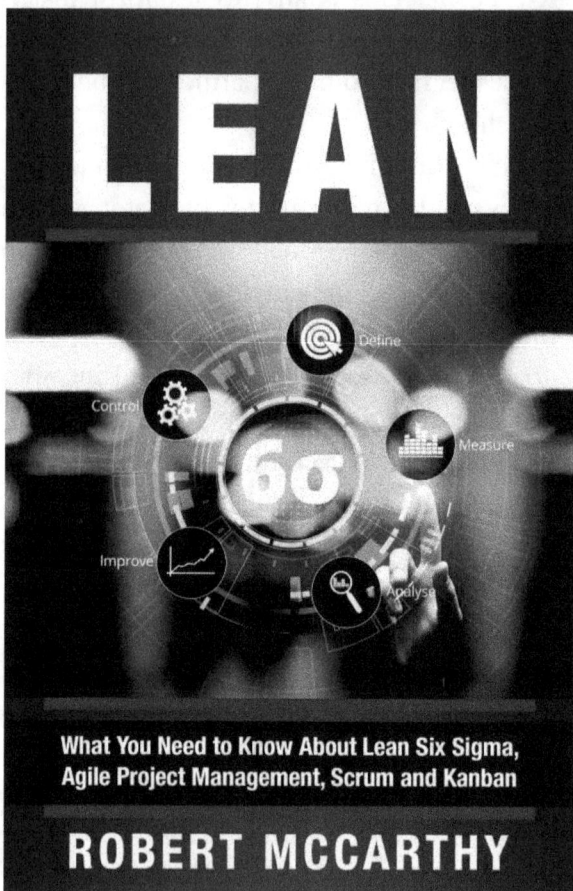

LEAN

What You Need to Know About Lean Six Sigma,
Agile Project Management, Scrum and Kanban

ROBERT MCCARTHY